From the Pope's Hand to Indigenous Lands

Law and Religion

Volumes published in this Brill Research Perspectives title are listed at *brill.com/rplrs*

From the Pope's Hand to Indigenous Lands

Alexander VI in Spanish Imperialism

By

Matthew P. Cavedon

BRILL

LEIDEN | BOSTON

Library Congress Control Number: 2023947508

Typeface for the Latin, Greek, and Cyrillic scripts: "Brill". See and download: brill.com/brill-typeface.

ISSN 2667-3398
ISBN 978-90-04-68142-2 (paperback)
ISBN 978-90-04-68143-9 (e-book)

This book is printed on acid-free paper and produced in a sustainable manner.

In order that you may enter upon so great an undertaking with greater readiness and heartiness endowed with the benefit of our apostolic favor, we, of our own accord, not at your instance nor the request of anyone else in your regard, but of our own sole largess and certain knowledge and out of the fullness of our apostolic power, by the authority of Almighty God conferred upon us in blessed Peter and of the vicarship of Jesus Christ, which we hold on earth, do by tenor of these presents, should any of said islands have been found by your envoys and captains, give, grant, and assign to you and your heirs and successors, kings of Castile and Leon, forever, together with all their dominions, cities, camps, places, and villages, and all rights, jurisdictions, and appurtenances, all islands and mainlands.

POPE ALEXANDER VI, "Inter caetera" (1493) (trans. FRANCES GARDINER DAVENPORT)

Contents

Acknowledgments

I thank my wife Julie for her constant love and patience. This work's preparation was invaluably aided by John Witte Jr., Justin Latterell, Rafael Domingo-Osle, Whittney Barth, Charles Reid Jr., Yuri Mantilla, Robert Miller, Robert A. Williams Jr., Gary Hauk, and Rafael Ramis Barceló. Essential research assistance came from Emory Law research librarians Amy Flick, Brady Beard, and Emily Corbin, Emory Law student Kameron St Clare, and Patrick Kerwin of the Library of Congress. I also thank Sam Gregg, Luis Girón-Negrón, and Br. Miguel Anxo Peña González for igniting my interest in the School of Salamanca years ago. Further inspiration for—and by my belief, intercession aiding—this book came from Servant of God Bartolomé de Las Casas, Saints Juan Diego and Kateri Tekakwitha, and Our Lady of Guadalupe. None of my work at the Center would be possible without the generous support of the McDonald Agape Foundation. Finally, thank you to the Brill team and the anonymous reviewers for making this book better.

From the Pope's Hand to Indigenous Lands

Alexander VI in Spanish Imperialism

Matthew P. Cavedon
Emory University, Atlanta, Georgia, USA
matthew.paul.cavedon@emory.edu

Abstract

In 1493, shortly after Christopher Columbus returned from his first voyage to the West Indies, Pope Alexander VI issued a bull known as *Inter caetera*. It authorized centuries of brutal conquest, according to many Indigenous activists and scholarly critics. It was a historically insignificant "remnant," according to some Catholic apologists. In truth, the bull's influence was complicated. Despite what many modern critics protest, *Inter caetera* had no role in English (or French, or Dutch) imperialism. However, Alexander likely did understand it as authorizing violent conquest, albeit of only a few islands. What is more, his words remained a central part of the Spanish Empire's self-justification for centuries. The bull retained prominence even after the rise of alternative natural-law theories of international order. For many imperialists and many colonial subjects, Spain received its right to rule Indigenous lands straight from the Pope's hand.

Keywords

Doctrine of discovery – colonialism – imperialism – Catholic – history – Spain – Vitoria – Las Casas – Pope Alexander VI

Inter caetera Introduced: Pope Francis Confronts Colonial History in Canada

In 1493, shortly after Christopher Columbus returned from his first voyage to the West Indies, Pope Alexander VI issued a bull known as *Inter caetera*. It authorized centuries of brutal conquest, according to many Indigenous activists and scholarly critics. It was a historically insignificant "remnant," according to some Catholic apologists.

 | DOI:10.1163/9789004681439_002

In truth, the bull's influence was complicated. Despite what many modern critics protest, *Inter caetera* had no role in English (or French, or Dutch) imperialism. However, Alexander likely did understand it as authorizing violent conquest, albeit of only a few islands. What is more, his words remained a central part of the Spanish Empire's self-justification for centuries. The bull retained prominence even after the rise of alternative natural-law theories of international order. For many imperialists and many colonial subjects, Spain received its right to rule Indigenous lands straight from the Pope's hand.

Pope Francis's summer of 2022 came to an uncomfortable end. He and the press corps were on a plane returning to Rome from Canada. The first Bishop of Rome from Latin America had just concluded a "penitential pilgrimage" apologizing for the Catholic Church's role in abuses against First Nations. An Indigenous journalist asked him whether he should have also rejected the so-called "Doctrine of Discovery." He responded that he did not know what she meant. This was seen as a "shocking" gaffe, as it followed years of high-profile demands by Indigenous activists.[1] Indeed, mere moments before a papal Mass at a Quebec basilica, protesters inside the sanctuary had unfurled a banner reading "RESCIND THE DOCTRINE."[2]

Some blamed the Pope's confusion on a lack of briefing.[3] That may be so, but his bafflement was not the most outlandish response. The historical role of the Papacy in justifying colonization is complicated. The Catholic Church played no direct role in inaugurating the English colonization of North America. But critics do have a point that the Holy See and some Catholic apologists have often denied: Pope Alexander VI (r. 1492–1503) may have fully intended to set the Kingdom of Castile off on the bloody adventure that became the Spanish Empire, and his words did become a major part of that power's self-justification.

In 1492, Christopher Columbus made landfall in the Caribbean, the first of his voyages sponsored by Queen Isabella of Castile (r. 1474–1504) and Ferdinand of Aragon, her consort king (r. Castile 1479–1516)—known as the "Catholic Monarchs."[4] Shortly after Columbus returned to Europe the following year,

1 Thomas Reese S.J., *Pope Francis Was Not Fully Briefed Prior to Canadian Visit*, Nat'l Catholic Reporter, Aug. 5, 2022, https://www.ncronline.org/news/opinion/pope-francis-was-not-fully-briefed-prior-canadian-visit.

2 Ricardo da Silva S.J., *Explainer: Could Pope Francis Revoke the 15th-Century 'Doctrine of Discovery' Used to Justify Colonizing Indigenous Peoples?*, America, July 28, 2022, https://www.americamagazine.org/politics-society/2022/07/28/dontrine-discovery-pope-francis-243435.

3 *See* Reese, *supra* n.1.

4 *See* Peter d'Errico, *Native Americans in America: A Theoretical and Historical Overview*, 14 Wicazo Sa Rev. 7, 13 (1999) ("[Columbus's] adventure was not sponsored by Spain but by the kingdoms of Castile and Leon, which were only in the process of becoming 'Spain'—a process that included the conquest of the Iberian Peninsula from the Moors, which would be fueled by wealth extracted from the 'new world.'"). For more on early modern Spanish

Alexander issued a bull, or formal document, entitled *Inter caetera* ("Among other," for its first two words).[5] Its legally significant language read that the Pope would "give, grant, and assign" to Castile and its successors "all islands and mainlands found and to be found" to the west and south of the Azores and Cabo Verde, including "all their dominions, cities, camps, places, and villages, and all rights, jurisdictions, and appurtenances."[6]

The meaning of this has become the subject of heated debate. Many Indigenous activists, and some scholars, have identified it as the basis for European colonization. Hence their desire for a modern-day papal denouncement of the bull. Some Catholics have answered that *Inter caetera* was a dead letter almost immediately. A fuller look at the history uncovers distinctions, ambiguities, and nuances.

I begin by discussing how *Inter caetera* is **remembered** in current controversy, then **complicate** that memory by explaining that there is no one "Doctrine of Discovery": *Inter caetera* was just one among a number of rationales Europeans used to justify imperialism. Next, I **situate** *Inter caetera* by exploring what Alexander could have understood the bull to mean given its

---

history, see William D. Phillips Jr. & Carla Rahn Phillips, A Concise History of Spain 107–272 (2d ed., Cambridge Univ. Press 2015); Peter Pierson, The History of Spain 45–73 (2d ed., Greenwood 2019); John Edwards, Ferdinand and Isabella: Profiles in Power (2014); Juan Pablo Fusi, Historia Mínima de España 72–90 (2012).

5 "Bull" takes its name from the Latin "*bulla*," or seal. There were actually two bulls called *Inter caetera*, issued months apart. *See* James Muldoon, Popes, Lawyers, and Infidels: The Church and the Non-Christian World, 1250–1550 137–39 (1979) [hereinafter "Popes"]; William Henry Scott, *Demythologizing the Papal Bull "Inter Caetera"*, 35 Philippine Stud. 348, 352–55 (1987); Alexander VI, *The Bull* Inter caetera (May 3, 1493), *reprinted in* European Treaties Bearing on the History of the United States and Its Dependencies 56–63 (Frances Gardiner Davenport ed., Carnegie Inst. of Wash. 1917) [hereinafter "*IC I*"]; Alexander VI, *The Bull* Inter caetera (May 4, 1493), *reprinted in id.* at 71–78 [hereinafter "*Inter caetera*"]; *see also* Alexander VI, *The Bull* Eximiae Devotionis (May 3, 1493), *reprinted in id.* at 64–70 (confirming *Inter caetera* and apparently backdated).

Ferdinand first requested a bull retroactively authorizing Columbus's voyage and confirming Castile's rights to newly discovered lands. This *Inter caetera's* geographic reach was less than that of its successor. *See generally IC I*. It was swiftly recalled, and the only *Inter caetera* that the world long knew was the second bull (which was backdated to appear older than it really was). *See* Alfonso García Gallo, *Las Bulas de Alejandro VI y el Ordenamiento Jurídico de la Expansión Portuguesa y Castellana en África e Indias*, 27 Anuario de Historia del Derecho Español 461, 469, 521–38 (1957) (noting Herman Vander Linden's 1916 dating of the first bull and discussing the two versions). Alfonso García Gallo hypothesizes that the different documents addressed different nuances of the relationship between Castile and Portugal in the New World. *See id.* at 594–607; *cf.* Javier Barrientos Grandon, Historia del Derecho Indiano del Descubrimiento Colombino a la Codificación 31 (2000).

I refer only to the second *Inter caetera* from here on. Davenport's reprints feature the original Latin, as well as her English translations.

6 *Inter caetera*, *supra* n.5, at 77; *see also id.* at 74 (the Latin).

canon-law, historical, and geopolitical contexts. I move on to the early debates regarding *Inter caetera*'s **interpretation** that took place in the West Indies and Spain. Then, I examine the arguments of theologian Francisco de Vitoria that followed. These are often seen as having shifted Spain's rationale for colonization to natural law, but consideration of later thinkers shows that the bull continued to be important. I explain also how Bartolomé de Las Casas **inverted** *Inter caetera* into a radical limit on imperialism. Finally, I **assess** *Inter caetera*'s role in history: while the Pope may not have anticipated it becoming a justification for global empire, he did grant it with conquest in mind. Many imperialists and many colonial subjects always thought Spain received its rule over Indigenous lands from Alexander's hand.

1 *Inter caetera* Remembered: Current Catholic-Indigenous Controversies

Alexander's bull has featured prominently in modern debates between the Catholic Church and critics of colonialism's legacy. I begin with a survey of recent disputes that are based on what people **remember** it to be. When modern scholars started looking into the rationales for European colonialism, *Inter caetera* was just one small part of a much broader story. But in recent decades, it has become a symbol for all European imperialism: the keystone of a "Doctrine of Discovery" used to subject much of the world to European rule. Some Catholics have responded by writing off the bull as a dead letter (although the Vatican did recently issue a new statement avoiding that approach). These current controversies give *Inter caetera*'s actual role in history relevance today.

Contemporary debate around the supposed Doctrine of Discovery arguably began in 1972, when Lakota scholar Vine Deloria Jr. penned an "Open Letter to the Heads of the Christian Churches in America."[7] He describes early modern Europeans coming to a "gradual consensus" around the belief that "the peoples inhabiting the western continents were to be treated with respect" but their rights were subject to limits defined by Europeans.[8] "Thinking themselves justified by the god they worshipped," European Christians began to colonize the rest of the world.[9] Deloria calls for a day when Indigenous peoples could become more than "mere appendages of the Christian Doctrine of Discovery."[10]

7 *Reprinted in* For This Land: Writings on Religion in America (1999).
8 *Id.* at 77.
9 *Id.* at 78.
10 *Id.* at 83.

Two years later, he wrote that this Doctrine articulated a right of Europeans to seize unoccupied lands.[11] He draws careful distinctions and discusses *Inter caetera* only briefly. He calls it a gift to Castile, but then notes that the 1494 Treaty of Tordesillas divided colonization rights between that kingdom and Portugal.[12] The bull was disregarded entirely by other European powers like England and France.[13] Deloria dates the Doctrine of Discovery's "genesis" to post-Tordesillas diplomacy, not *Inter caetera*.[14]

Such nuance is missing from much recent commentary, which has often conflated *Inter caetera* with later U.S. doctrines of discovery.[15] Unfortunately, Deloria's later work falls into that trap. In an essay published posthumously in 2006, he characterizes the United States as having adopted the "nefarious" Doctrine of Discovery "articulated in" *Inter caetera*.[16] He breezily concludes that "[t]he belief that God appointed the Pope to rule over planet earth until the Second Coming of Jesus produced for many of the world's people a kind of legal limbo where justice could not be served, nor was it ever intended to be."[17]

Much had changed. Activist criticisms of *Inter caetera* "galvanized" in 1992, the five-hundredth anniversary of Columbus's first expedition.[18] That year, the Traditional Council of Indian Elders and Youth: (1) identified *Inter caetera* as a foundation of U.S. Indian law; (2) stated that the colonization of the future United States ultimately "rests upon" *Inter caetera*; and (3) called on Pope John Paul II to repudiate the bull.[19] A 1994 Declaration of Vision endorsed by the Onondaga Nation similarly identifies *Inter caetera* with U.S. Indian law, calling the bull "devastating to our religions, our cultures, and the survival of our populations."[20] In a 2017 article expressing the views of the Onondaga Council

---

11 Vine Deloria Jr., Behind the Trail of Broken Treaties: An Indian Declaration of Independence 85 (1974).

12 *Id.* at 87–88.

13 *Id.* at 88.

14 *Id.*

15 In this work, "American" refers to the continents and their Indigenous peoples.

16 Vine Deloria Jr., *Conquest Masquerading as Law*, in Unlearning the Language of Conquest: Scholars Expose Anti-Indianism in America, at 96 (Don Trent Jacobs ed., 2006).

17 *Id.* at 106–07.

18 See Baron Pineda, *Indigenous Pan-Americanism: Contesting Settler Colonialism and the Doctrine of Discovery at the UN Permanent Forum on Indigenous Issues*, 69 Am. Q. 823, 825–26 (2017).

19 Trad. Council of Indian Elders & Youth, Communique No. 15, Discovery—Heathens—Slavery—Religious Freedoms 1492–1992 (1992), *appendix to* Steven T. Newcomb, *The Evidence of Christian Nationalism in Federal Indian Law: The Doctrine of Discovery,* Johnson v. McIntosh, *and Plenary Power*, 20 NYU Rev. L. & Soc. Change 303, 340–41 (1993) [hereinafter "*Evidence*"].

20 *Declaration of Vision: Toward the Next 500 Years*, Turtle Q., Fall–Winter 1994, at 8, *quoted in* Joseph J. Heath, *The Doctrine of Christian Discovery: Its Fundamental Importance and the Need for Its Repudiation and Removal*, 10 Alb. Gov't L. Rev. 112, 122–23 (2017).

of Chiefs, Joseph J. Heath says that the English "adopted" *Inter caetera.*[21] He expresses confidence that the bull's condemnation by a modern pope would "remove[]" moral cover for U.S. Indian law.[22]

The following year, Canada's Assembly of First Nations stated: "Discovery started with the Pope and First Nations are owed the respect of having the Pope himself apologize."[23] That country's official Truth and Reconciliation Commission has described the Doctrine of Discovery as "having smoothly and relatively uncritically transitioned from Roman Catholic to international law."[24] Religion scholar Jennifer Reid took *Inter caetera* to be "the legal foundation upon which North America was colonized," defining "the limits of all land claims to this day and, more fundamentally, the necessity of land claims at all."[25] Across the Pacific, Māori activist Tina Ngata recently accused *Inter caetera* of giving "the monarchies of Britain and Europe the right to conquer and claim lands, and to convert or kill the native inhabitants."[26] Before Pope Francis visited Canada, Dehcho Grand Chief Stanley Sanguez said that the Catholic Church "started this whole [colonization] thing, and they have to end it."[27] The bull has become an icon of original evil for many activists.[28] In one

21 Heath, *supra* n.20, at 116–17, 120.

22 *Id.* at 156.

23 Assembly of First Nations, *Dismantling the Doctrine of Discovery*, at 6 (2018), *available at* https://www.afn.ca/wp-content/uploads/2018/02/18-01-22-Dismantling-the-Doctrine-of-Discovery-EN.pdf.

24 Truth & Recon. Comm'n of Can., Honouring the Truth, Reconciling for the Future 192 (2015), *available at* https://ehprnh2mwo3.exactdn.com/wp-content/uploads/2021/01/Executive_Summary_English_Web.pdf (*quoting* Jennifer Reid, *The Roman Catholic Foundations of Land Claims in Canada*, at 5–6 (Can. Soc'y of Church Hist., Historical Papers 2009), *available at* http://pi.library.yorku.ca/ojs/index.php/historicalpapers/article/viewFile/39133/35490).

25 Reid, *supra* n.24, at 6, 9.

26 Tina Ngata, *The Right to Conquer and Claim: Captain Cook and the Doctrine of Discovery*, The Spinoff, Oct. 3, 2019, https://thespinoff.co.nz/atea/03-10-2019/the-right-to-conquer-and-claim-captain-cook-and-the-doctrine-of-discovery.

27 *Pope's Apology Meaningless without Rescinding Doctrine of Discovery, Says Dehcho First Nations*, CBC News, Jun. 11, 2022, https://www.cbc.ca/news/canada/north/dehcho-first-nations-doctrine-of-discovery-1.6484337; *see also* Andrea Smith, *Boarding School Abuses, Human Rights, and Reparations*, 31 Soc. Just. 89, 97 (2004) ("Another possible remedy would be to get the Catholic Church to rescind the papal bulls that set the legal precedents in the U.S. for the doctrine of discovery .... [which] would potentially undermine U.S. legal claims over our land since U.S. case law is based on these papal bulls.").

28 *See* Pineda, *supra* n.19, at 830 (arguing that campaigning around *Inter caetera* helps "Latin American indigenous activists to avoid the pitfalls of a 'liberal inclusion'"); Jean-François Roussel, *Doctrine de la Découverte: Préciser les Enjeux Théologiques d'une Revendication Autochtone*, 51 Stud. in Religion/Sciences Religieuses 3, 23 (2022) ("Même si la doctrine de la découverte était annulée de fait, et ... est devenue aujourd'hui ["Even if the doctrine of discovery has been effectively annulled, and ... has become today] 'a dogmatic body of

particularly dramatic flourish in 2016, an Episcopalian priest in North Dakota presided over a ritual burning of *Inter caetera* in front of hundreds of cheering protesters and clerics.[29]

Alexander's bull has also been a focus of Indigenous-Catholic dialogue. In 2007, a Native American delegation requested a formal response to the bull from the Holy See's United Nations mission.[30] In 2010, the mission tersely wrote that the Treaty of Tordesillas, and other historical and legal changes, abrogated the bull long ago.[31] It described *Inter caetera* as "a historic remnant with no juridical, moral or doctrinal value" and said the Church has ascribed it "no value whatsoever for centuries."[32] In 2016, Canada's Catholic bishops issued a similar statement, framing *Inter caetera* "more as a missionary document than as a political one."[33]

Some other Catholics have bought into this attitude as well. Andrew Boyd recently wrote that demanding more from the Vatican is "a bit like asking Queen Elizabeth II to revoke Jim Crow or Prohibition in the U.S.," because the Doctrine of Discovery "is a) not primarily the pope's to begin with, b) has been 'revoked' already, condemned, and rejected repeatedly over centuries,

---

shared theories (informing theory, law, and understanding) pertaining to the rightfulness and righteousness of settler belief systems and the supremacy of the institutions (legal, economic, governmental) that are based upon those belief systems', le substrat biblique et chrétien demeure l'une des sources qui contribuent á l'orienter et à la légitimer [the biblical and Christian substrate remains the source that contributes the most to its orientation and legitimation]." (*quoting* T. Lindberg, *The Doctrine of Discovery in Canada*, in Discovering Indigenous Lands: The Doctrine of Discovery in the English Colonies 94 (Robert J. Miller et al., eds. 2010) [hereinafter "Discovering"]). Translations are mine (with assistance from ChatGPT, an artificial intelligence model) unless otherwise noted. *See* OpenAI, ChatGPT, https://www.openai.com.

29 *See* Pineda, *supra* n.18, at 823.

30 *See* Vinnie Rotondaro, *Doctrine of Discovery: A Scandal in Plain Sight*, Nat'l Catholic Rep., Sept. 5, 2015, https://www.ncronline.org/doctrine-discovery-scandal-plain-sight.

31 Perm. Obs. Miss. of the Holy See, Statement on Agenda Item 7: Discussion on the Reports "Impact on Indigenous Peoples of the International Legal Construct Known as the Doctrine of Discovery, Which Has Served as the Foundation of the Violation of Their Human Rights" and "Indigenous Peoples and Boarding Schools: A Comparative Study", at 1, delivered to the Economic and Social Council, 9th Session of the Permanent Forum on Indigenous Issues, Apr. 27, 2010, *available at* https://www.cccb.ca/wp-content/uploads/2020/01/Holy-See.pdf.

32 *Id.* at 2.

33 *See* Can. Conf. of Catholic Bishops, *The "Doctrine of Discovery" and* Terra Nullius: *A Catholic Response* at 10–11 (Mar. 19, 2016), *available at* https://www.cccb.ca/wp-content/uploads /2017/11/catholic-response-to-doctrine-of-discovery-and-tn.pdf.

and c) is not 'still on the books' in any way, even as a technicality."[34] He said that *Inter caetera* was "barely in effect for thirteen months" before the Treaty of Tordesillas.[35] Besides, it lacks "any excuse or justification for slavery, the deprivation of properties and freedoms, or inhumane treatment."[36]

Protests have not stopped, though. They have even reached the highest levels of Church hierarchy. In 2016, a Pan-American Indigenous delegation asked Pope Francis to renounce the Doctrine of Discovery.[37] His Canada pilgrimage finally triggered a formal response: in March 2023, two Vatican offices issued a joint statement describing *Inter caetera* as "written in a specific historical period and linked to political questions" and then "manipulated for political purposes by competing colonial powers."[38]

Whether this statement is adequate is ultimately a question for further Indigenous-Catholic dialogue. What is beyond dispute is the endurance of controversy over *Inter caetera*: over the past fifty years, it has gone from an academic sidenote to a major flashpoint. Indigenous activists and scholars identify it as one of imperialism's driving engines. Many Catholic commentators, if not the most recent Vatican statement, have tried to downplay it. One side says Alexander gave Castile the world. The other says Spain mutilated a minor legal document into a major ideological piece.

Neither side gets the history right. I first dissect one of the critics' main arguments: that *Inter caetera* inspired one pan-European Doctrine of Discovery. This claim is powerful because it is simple and identifies the Catholic Church as a target for universal anti-colonialist activism. This claim is also wrong.

---

34 Andrew Boyd, *Papal Condemnation of the Doctrine of Discovery*, Church Life J., Aug. 30, 2022, https://churchlifejournal.nd.edu/articles/papal-condemnation-of-the-doctrine-of-discovery/.

35 *Id.*

36 *Id.*

37 *See* Pineda, *supra* n.18, at 826.

38 Dicasteries for Culture and Education and for Promoting Integral Human Development, *Joint Statement on the "Doctrine of Discovery,"* para. 6, Daily Bulletin (Mar. 30, 2023), *available at* https://press.vatican.va/content/salastampa/en/bollettino.html. The statement also denies that *Inter caetera* is "part of" Catholic teaching and "acknowledges" that it "did not adequately reflect the equal dignity and rights of indigenous peoples." *Id.* The statement recognizes "these errors" and "the pain experienced by indigenous peoples," seeking "pardon." *Id.* It "repudiates ... the legal and political 'doctrine of discovery.'" *Id.* para. 7.

2 *Inter caetera* Complicated: the Plural Rationales for European Colonization

History is more **complicated** than many critics recognize. There was no one Doctrine of Discovery built from Alexander's bull. Instead, at least four different doctrines were used to justify European imperialism: (1) *Inter caetera*'s; (2) Spanish theologian Francisco de Vitoria's (more on him below); (3) the U.S. Supreme Court's as articulated in the 1820s; and (4) a radical British theory that Australia was uninhabited. Part of the modern confusion about *Inter caetera*'s role stems from errors made by early U.S. judges. But critics put too much blame on Alexander for colonization by many European empires; *Inter caetera* was even condemned as unjust by the English.

There was no one Doctrine of Discovery. As Deloria noted, different rationales for colonization were used by different empires in different eras. Douglas Lind recently published a comprehensive overview.[39] He notes that several decades after *Inter caetera*, Spanish Dominican theologian Francisco de Vitoria (*c.*1486–1546) proposed a "natural law right of discovery" with important differences from the bull.[40] In turn, the doctrine later proposed by influential Swiss theorist Emer de Vattel (1714–1767) "directly contradicted" Vitoria and moved farther away from Catholic theories.[41] The earlier Dutch jurist Hugo Grotius (1583–1645) had rejected any papal authority over non-Christians—a position overlapping somewhat with Vitoria's, but incompatible with *Inter caetera*.[42] Then, the doctrine of discovery articulated by the U.S. Supreme Court in the 1820s–30s was based more on innovation than on an accurate reading of history.[43] There was also a radical British theory that aboriginal peoples did not effectively "inhabit" Australia.[44] As Lind writes, collapsing these into one

39 Douglas Lind, *Doctrines of Discovery*, 13 Wash. U. Jurisprudence Rev. 1, 8 (2020). Parts of this section overlap with my article *Did Pope Alexander VI Authorize England's Colonization of North America?*, Canopy Forum, March 21, 2023, https://canopyforum.org/2023/03/21/did-pope-alexander-vi-authorize-englands-colonization-of-north-america/.

40 Lind, *supra* n.39, at 8.

41 *Id.*

42 *See* David M. Lantigua, Infidels and Empires in a New World Order 200–01 (2020).

43 Lind, *supra* n.39, at 8.

44 *Id.* at 9. "The British in Australia … justif[ied] the seizure of occupied land if the indigenous inhabitants, through English eyes, were so barbarous and low on the scale of civil polity that their cultural attachments to land could be wholly disregarded." *Id.* at 49. Spaniards never characterized the Americas as uninhabited. See Anthony Pagden, Lords of All the World: Ideologies of Empire in Spain, Britain and France *c.*1500–*c.*1800 91 (1995) [hereinafter "Lords"].

"doctrine" "misrepresents jurisprudential history, generates needless theoretical confusion, and undermines future efforts to rectify past injustices."[45]

One of the greatest historical mistakes is blaming *Inter caetera* for English, U.S., and French colonization. As Lind says, "the papal theory only nominally impacted" powers other than Spain and Portugal.[46] A rejection of Alexander's bull begins almost every "French or English attack on the claims to Spanish sovereignty overseas."[47] Christianity certainly had a role in other empires, and Catholic canon-law precedent both undergirded *Inter caetera* and contributed to wider European thought.[48] But the bull itself was "wholly severed" from most imperial ideologies.[49] French King Francis I mockingly said in 1540 that he would not accept the bull without first seeing "Adam's will."[50] Later

45 Lind, *supra* n.39, at 9.

46 *Id.* at 18; *see also* Pagden, Lords, *supra* n.44, at 47 ("The arguments directed against the Bulls by the English and the French depended upon a denial of the Papacy's implicit assumption of jurisdiction. ... Furthermore, as the British pointed out, even if the donation were held to be legitimate by Catholics, it would not be binding on Protestants.").

47 Pagden, Lords, *supra* n.44, at 48.

48 Lumbee legal scholar Robert A. Williams made this helpful observation in corresponding with me about a draft of this work. *See* Part 3 *infra*; Han Liu, *The Pre-History of Self-Determination: Union and Disunion of States in Early Modern International Law*, 36 Ariz. J. Int'l & Comp. L. 1, 35 (2019) ("[B]ased on the principle that the state should cultivate the land, Vattel argued that the Indian tribes occupied, but did not own the land of America. ... This represents the typical Protestant justification ...."); Pagden, Lords, *supra* n.44, at 35 ("Even the English ... made their earliest claim to legitimacy in the name of the seemingly implausible obligation to convert the heathen to the faith."); Ward Churchill, *Perversions of Justice: Examining the Doctrine of U.S. Rights to Occupancy in North America*, 21 Hist. Reflections 319, 324 (1995) ("... England had already begun to mark its independence from papal regulation by adding an element of its own to the doctrine. Usually termed the 'Norman Yoke,' this concept asserted that land rights depend in large part upon the extent to which the owners demonstrate a willingness and ability to 'develop' their territories in accordance with a scriptual [sic] obligation to exercise 'dominion' over nature."). Note controversies regarding Churchill. *See* Ward Churchill, On the Justice of Roosting Chickens: Reflections on the Consequences of U.S. Imperial Arrogance and Criminality 33 n.126 (2003) (acknowledging his comparison of 9/11 victims to Nazis); Wes Enzinna, *"I Never Claimed I Was F***ing Sitting Bull"*, Mother Jones, Sept. 5, 2017, https://www.motherjones.com/politics/2017/09/professor-ward-churchill-native-american-comeback/ (discussing disputes over his claimed Indigenous ancestry).

49 Lind, *supra* n.40, at 23.

50 James Muldoon, *Colonial Charters: Possessory or Regulatory?*, 36 L. & Hist. Rev. 355, 366 (2018) [hereinafter "*Colonial Charters*"]. France actually invaded parts of Italy and threatened Alexander's control of Rome for reasons unrelated to *Inter caetera*, although the two sides later reconciled. *See* 3 Mandell Creighton, A History of the Papacy During the Period of the Reformation: The Italian Princes 1464–1518 pp. 183–214, 249, 264–70 (1887). Later on, France devised "very creative" arguments for limiting *Inter caetera*. Robert J. Miller et al., *The International Law of Discovery, Indigenous Peoples, and Chile*, 89 Neb. L. Rev. 819, 847 (2011) [hereinafter "*Chile*"].

English writers accused Spain of deriving "rights of conquest from the supposed ungodliness of non-Christians."[51]

Indigenous activists, then, incorrectly blame Alexander for the colonization of Canada, Australia, New Zealand, and much of the United States.[52] In fairness, so did some nineteenth-century American jurists, especially in Tennessee (then an Anglo-Cherokee borderland).[53] But they were mistaken. Anthony Pagden observes that King Henry VII's letters patent authorizing John Cabot's 1496 voyage for England "were to some degree an attempt to replicate the language of papal legislation, as were the grants made by Elizabeth I to Sir Walter Raleigh in March 1584. But for all their assumed authority neither

51 Anthony Pagden, *Law, Colonization, Legitimation, and the European Background*, in 1 Cambridge History of Law in America: Early America (1580–1815) at 8 (Michael Grossberg & Christopher Tomlins eds., 2008) [hereinafter "*European Background*"].

52 Regarding British and U.S. colonization in the Pacific, see Stuart Banner, Possessing the Pacific: Land, Settlers, and Indigenous People from Australia to Alaska (2007). *Inter caetera is* relevant to parts of the United States that were colonized by the Spanish. *See United States v. Santa Fe P.R. Co.*, 314 U.S. 339, 364 (1941) (holding Indian land title to be protected under the Mexican Cession because of Spanish law); Felix S. Cohen, *The Spanish Origin of Indian Rights in the Law of the United States*, 31 Geo. L.J. 1, 18 (1942) ("[T]he use of Spanish authorities is a result of the fact that most of the territory of the United States was once under Spanish dominion.").

53 *See generally* J.M. Opal, *General Jackson's Passports: Natural Rights and Sovereign Citizens in the Political Thought of Andrew Jackson, 1780s–1820s*, 27 Stud. in Am. Pol. Dev. 69 (2013); *State v. Foreman*, 16 Tenn. 256, 277–78 (1835) ("[T]he principle declared in the fifteenth century as the law of Christendom, that discovery gave title to assume sovereignty over, and to govern the unconverted natives of Africa, Asia, and North and South America, has been recognized as a part of the national law, for nearly four centuries, and ... it is now so recognized by every Christian power .... [I]t is our duty not to shrink from a principle on which the title and value of Louisiana depend ... because the Popes of Rome made, and by the force of their once sovereign authority, established it. Its promulgation may have been a harsh fiat, and it may have been cruelly executed by the Spaniards in Peru and Mexico; yet it is the fiat of our recognition, from the Catholic reign of Henry the Seventh, through every change of religion and government in England, by the colonies up to the revolution, and the States having Indian relations since."); *Cornet v. Winston's Lessee*, 10 Tenn. 143, 152 (1826) ("To have a correct view of the rules adopted and applied to Indian affairs when grants were issued by the Kings of England for lands in North America, we must look to the prevailing opinions of those days in matters of religion. The spiritual father of christendom dictated the creed of the people .... As the successor of St. Peter, [the pope's] grants of infidel countries were considered binding in heaven, and of course, upon the consciences of christians.").

Even back then, some jurists knew better. See *Foreman*, 16 Tenn. at 343 (Green, J., concurring) (describing the papal bulls as "never maintained by the English monarchs, nor practised upon by the colonists from that country; but ... condemned by all Protestant writers ....").

Henry nor Elizabeth were pontiffs[.]"[54] Cabot's letters patent do not mention *Inter caetera*.[55] Later English imperialists were Protestants who rejected papal authority entirely. In 1584, Richard Hakluyt called *Inter caetera* a "most unreasonable and injurious donation."[56] "A representative of Henry VII's Protestant granddaughter, Elizabeth I ([r.] 1558–1603), bluntly told Spain's ambassador that 'the Pope had no right to partition the world and to give and take kingdoms to whomsoever he pleased.'"[57] Promoting Virginia's colonization in 1609, Robert Johnson made short shrift of the bull: "what is it to us?"[58] Later U.S. discussion of the Doctrine of Discovery is convoluted, partly because Chief Justice John Marshall badly mischaracterized legal history in the seminal 1823 decision *Johnson v. M'Intosh*. But at least *Johnson* correctly set aside *Inter caetera*.[59]

Inter caetera did not drive all European colonization. It was even derided as unjust by the English. Their own imperialism certainly had Christian reasoning behind it too, but to blame Alexander for the Mayflower is to follow errors made by a handful of early U.S. judges. This is to the detriment of activists' arguments. As Lind writes, when European colonizers are misremembered as "a cultural monolith pursuing a grand plan," "injustice cannot be repaired—land claims fairly adjudicated—[and] the case for reparations fully made" because "the precise terms of the American Indians' dispossession of their lands" are distorted.[60]

However, some Catholic officials and writers tack to the opposite extreme and deny that *Inter caetera* lent support to conquest anywhere. That, too, is mistaken. Careful consideration of the bull's original contexts shows that

54 Pagden, *European Background*, *supra* n.51, at 5; *see also* Muldoon, *Colonial Charters*, *supra* n.50, at 358.

55 *See generally Patent Granted by King Henry VII to John Cabot and His Sons, March 1496* (John F. Flinn trans., 1982), *available at* https://www.heritage.nf.ca/articles/exploration/1496-cabot-patent.php; Muldoon, *Colonial Charters*, *supra* n.51, at 368–69.

56 Lantigua, *supra* n.42, at 199.

57 James Muldoon, The Americas in the Spanish World Order: The Justification for Conquest in the Seventeenth Century 98 (2015) [hereinafter "Americas"].

58 Robert Johnson, Nova Britannia: Offering Most Excellent Fruits by Planting in Virginia; Exciting All Such as Be Well Affected to Further the Same (1609), *reprinted in* 6 Am. Colonial Tracts Monthly, at 4 (1897).

59 *See* 21 U.S. 543, 574 (stating only, and incorrectly: "Spain did not rest her title solely on the grant of the Pope. ... [S]he placed it on the rights given by discovery."); Lind, *supra* n.39, at 45 ("The only commonality between Marshall's principle and the papal theory ... is the bare concept of discovery. ... He ignored [the Papacy] entirely in *Worcester* [*v. Georgia*, 31 U.S. 515 (1832)]."). For a sharply critical history of *Johnson*, see Lindsay Robertson, Conquest by Law: How the Discovery of America Dispossessed Indigenous Peoples of Their Lands (2005).

60 Lind, *supra* n.39, at 59, 63.

Alexander can plausibly be accused of giving to Castile a right to dominate Indigenous peoples.

3 *Inter caetera* Situated: Canonical, Historical, and Geopolitical Contexts

Before addressing how Spaniards used *Inter caetera*, it is important to **situate** it contextually. The bull capped a pyramid of canon-law thought that had begun to rise at least three centuries earlier. It responded to historical events whose significance had not yet been fully appreciated. But it was a conscious part of papal geopolitics. It did sanction some imperialism, though the full extent of what Europeans had discovered across the Atlantic remained unknown.

3.1 *Canon Law: the Question of Non-Christian* **dominium**

Franciscan friar John of Plano Carpini (*c.*1180–1252) was around sixty-five years old when he went on one of history's least-expected missions.[61] The Mongol Horde had appeared on Europe's horizons. Friar John's three-thousand-mile task was to meet its great khan, evangelize him, and warn him that he was sinning by invading Christian lands.[62]

Friar John did not defuse the threat, but his endeavor was daring and based on doctrines relevant for understanding *Inter caetera*.[63] His mission reflected new ideas about non-Christians within canon law (the law governing the Catholic Church's institutional affairs). The pope he served under, Innocent IV (r. 1243–1254), was about to propose radical new theories about the political authority of "infidels" (non-believers) within their own societies. But Innocent also left the door open to wars against them, and an influential student of his, Henricus de Segusio ("Hostiensis") (*c.*1200–1271), would even argue that the Church can conquer infidels at any time. Their ideas framed pre-Columbus colonization ranging from Lithuania to the Canary Islands, and Ireland to the

61 Sophie Andrade, *The Franciscan Friar Who Went to the Mongol Empire*, Medievalists.net, https://www.medievalists.net/2021/05/the-franciscan-friar-who-went-to-the-mongol-empire/.

62 Eila M.J. Campbell, *Giovanni da Pian del Carpini*, Britannica, https://www.britannica.com/biography/Giovanni-da-Pian-del-Carpini.

63 James Muldoon, *Papal Responsibility for the Infidel: Another Look at Alexander VI's "Inter Caetera"*, 64 Catholic Hist. Rev. 168, 170, 172 (1978) [hereinafter "*Papal Responsibility*"]. John wrote extensively and became a "very popular" speaker about the Mongols, praising their virtues. Mirko Sardelić, *John of Plano Carpini vs Simon of Saint-Quentin: 13th-Century Emotions in the Eurasian Steppe*, 5 Golden Horde Rev. 494, 498, 500 (2017). He died an archbishop. *See* Campbell, *supra* n.62.

coast of West Africa. These theories provided key **canonical context** for *Inter caetera*: legally speaking, the pope could authorize Christian rulers to conquer others and could set limits on those endeavors.

Prior to Innocent's day, Christians divided the rest of humanity into four categories: "the schismatic, heretic, Jew, or Saracen"—"each of whom posed a threat."[64] Canon-law scholars mainly thought about them in terms of just-war theory or as non-believers living within Christendom; canonists gave relatively little attention to infidels abroad.[65] Incredibly, it was the Mongols who caused churchmen to contemplate "the possibility of peaceful relations with non-Christian societies."[66] And Friar John, not crusaders, was sent to meet these new arrivals.

Contemplating the Mongols from comfier confines, Innocent proposed that infidels—because they were potential Christians—merited his pastoral solicitude.[67] This idea of universal papal responsibilities had ancient precedent, partly in the form of the "Donation of Constantine," by which the popes supposedly received the right to rule (*imperium*) over much of the western Roman Empire in the fourth century.[68] The Donation was shown to be a forgery as early as 1440 (though it had prominence in Spanish thought until as late as 1655).[69] According to Pagden, it meant that "[*d*]*e facto* there might

---

64 Muldoon, *Papal Responsibility*, *supra* n.63, at 170.

65 *Id.*; *see also* Muldoon, Popes, *supra* n.5, at 5 ("An extended discussion of the crusades might have led the canonists to a general consideration of the relations that could exist between Christian and non-Christian societies, leading, perhaps, to a theory of international relations .... From the point of view of the canonists, there was no reason to develop a theory of relations between Christians and those infidels who lived outside of Christian Europe because the Church, as opposed to individual Christian states, had no reason to enter into relations with infidel states."). However, canonists had started thinking about infidel marriage. *See* Charles J. Reid Jr., *Toward an Understanding of Medieval Universal Rights: The Marital Rights of Non-Christians in Early Scholastic and Canonistic Writings*, 3 Ave Maria L. Rev. 95, 96 (2005).

66 Muldoon, *Papal Responsibility*, *supra* n.63, at 170.

67 *Id.* at 171–72. For more regarding Innocent, see Kathleen G. Cushing, *Sinibaldo Fieschi (Pope Innocent IV) (1180/90–1254)*, in Law and the Christian Tradition in Italy: The Legacy of the Great Jurists 70 *et seq.* (Orazio Condorelli & Rafael Domingo eds., 2020).

68 *See* Liu, *supra* n.48, at 12; Pagden, Lords, *supra* n.44, at 26–27 ("[I]t was argued, the empire Jupiter had founded and Augustus had recreated had then passed through a succession of political translations to Constantine the Great, and Constantine—at least in the fertile political imagination of the eighth century Papacy—had bequeathed imperium (now conceived as a quasi hereditary property) to the Papacy and the Papacy had bestowed it upon a succession of Germanic rulers."). Hence the Germanic identification of their sovereigns as "emperors."

69 Pagden, Lords, *supra* n.44, at 32; *see also* Emily O'Brien, The *Commentaries* of Pope Pius II (1458–1464) and the Crisis of the Fifteenth-Century Papacy 40 (2015).

exist other kings in the world, just as *de facto* there existed other belief systems besides Christianity. But *de iure*, there could be only one emperor and only one religion."[70] And only one pope to care for all of humanity.

Innocent taught that the Church should exercise that care by evangelizing peacefully and that coexistence with infidels was possible.[71] He also recognized that they held *dominium* (ownership over labor, possessions, land, and politics) by natural right.[72] But this was subject to important limits that would later influence *Inter caetera*. If a non-Christian ruler forbade evangelization or oppressed converts, the pope could ask Christian sovereigns to intervene.[73] Innocent also believed that Jesus Christ gave the pope the "divine power and jurisdictional authority" to depose rulers.[74] This power extended everywhere

70 Pagden, Lords, *supra* n.44, at 27.

71 *See* Muldoon, *Papal Responsibility*, *supra* n.63, at 172.

72 *See id.*; Lantigua, *supra* n.42, at 38; James Muldoon, Extra Ecclesiam Non Est Imperium: *The Canonists and the Legitimacy of Secular Power*, 9 Studia Gratiana 553, 570–80 (1966) [hereinafter "*Extra Ecclesiam*"]. For more detailed discussions of *dominium*, see Anthony Pagden, *Dispossessing the Barbarian: The Language of Spanish Thomism and the Debate Over the Property Rights of American Indians*, in The Languages of Political Theory in Early-Modern Europe 79–98 (1987) [hereinafter "*Dispossessing*"]; Olive P. Dickason, *Concepts of Sovereignty at the Time of First Contacts*, in The Law of Nations and the New World 146–50 (L.C. Green & Olive Dickason eds., 1993); Virpi Mäkinen & Mikko Posti, *Whether Heretics and Infidels Can Possess Dominion Rights? Late Medieval and Early Modern Debates*, in A Companion to Early Modern Spanish Imperial Political and Social Thought 174 (Jörg Tellkamp ed., 2020) ("[*Dominium*] could refer to property, but it could also stand for any legal power and authority of different agents: kings, people, bishops, fathers, or property holders. ... [D]ominion came to be treated as the same thing as *ius*, a right ....").

73 Muldoon, *Papal Responsibility*, *supra* n.63, at 172.

74 Lantigua, *supra* n.42, at 40. Popes also claimed this power over Christian societies. *See* Muldoon, *Colonial Charters*, *supra* n.50, at 377 (discussing the English-born Pope Adrian IV's supposed 1155 bull *Laudabiliter*, authorizing England's colonization of Ireland); Muldoon, Americas, *supra* n.57, at 132–33 ("No one would deny the pope's right to restore proper ecclesiastical discipline to a Christian people who had gone astray, although some might quarrel with the transfer of the government of Ireland from the native rulers to Henry II."); Boris Milinković, *The Relationship between Church and State in the Medieval Document* Dictatus Papae, 32 Istraživanja/J. Hist. Researches 233, 236 (2021) (describing Pope Gregory VII's eleventh-century assertion of the authority to depose rulers); *but see* Marie Therese Flanagan, *Laudabiliter*, in The Oxford Companion to Irish History (2d ed., S.J. Connolly ed., 2002) (noting controversy over *Laudabiliter's* authenticity). The Spaniard Juan de Solórzano Pereira, whom I discuss in Part 4.3.2 below, called the English hypocrites for claiming Ireland based on *Laudabiliter* while rejecting *Inter caetera*. *See* Muldoon, Americas, *supra* n.58, at 134. During her short Catholic reign (1553–1558), England's Queen Mary Tudor secured papal confirmation of her rule over Ireland. *See* Robert J. Miller, *The Doctrine of Discovery*, in Miller et al., Discovering, *supra* n.28, at 16. Her husband was Spain's King Philip II.

precisely because the pope was responsible for everyone's welfare.[75] A ruler could be deposed for tolerating idolatry—not because it is un-Christian, but because it violates natural law.[76]

David Lantigua writes that this view came to hold "singular importance": "Applied to non-Christian societies where religion and political life were inseparable, Innocent's rationale for intervention outlined a doctrine of missionary warfare."[77] Innocent did distinguish between "direct and indirect forms of coercion," only approving of the latter—but that category was broad, including even forcing Jews to listen to Christian sermons because "the force of law and fear of punishment" could "remove obstacles" to conversion.[78] Foreshadowing a key element of the Spanish document known as the "*Requerimiento*," which I discuss below, Innocent thought that infidels who rejected papal authority "should fear the threat of war and slavery."[79]

Balancing this, though, Innocent's response to the Mongol Horde was to send the peaceful Friar John.[80] In authorizing war, Innocent was mainly thinking of Christian-Muslim conflicts in the Holy Land.[81] He reserved to the Papacy the right to declare religious wars, insisting on "supreme discretion" and "extreme conditions."[82] He accepted tolerant non-Christian rulers retaining civil authority over Christian converts.[83] Tolerance toward peaceful nonbelievers "remained the political norm."[84]

---

75 *See* Lantigua, *supra* n.42, at 39.

76 *See id.* at 39–40.

77 *Id.*; *see also* James Muldoon, *John Wyclif and the Rights of the Infidels: The Requerimiento Re-Examined*, 36 Americas 301, 312 (1980) [hereinafter "*Requerimiento*"] (explaining that Innocent "essentially admitted the right of Christians to invade infidel societies" and created "a scale of spiritual priorities which the pope could invoke to override the *dominium* of infidels").

78 Lantigua, *supra* n.42, at 40. The prohibition of direct coercion retained force; the Catholic Church also ultimately rejected indirect coercion in the twentieth century. Pagden, Lords, *supra* n.44, at 31; *see also* Pope Paul VI, *Declaration on Religious Freedom* Dignitatis Humanae (Dec. 7, 1965), *available at* https://www.vatican.va/archive/hist_councils/ii_vatican_council/documents/vat-ii_decl_19651207_dignitatis-humanae_en.html.

79 Lantigua, *supra* n.42, at 41.

80 *See* Muldoon, *Extra Ecclesiam*, *supra* n.72, at 580.

81 *See* Lantigua, *supra* n.42, at 42; Muldoon, *Requerimiento*, *supra* n.77, at 304 ("Wars to gain other Moslem territories would be wars of aggression and therefore forbidden."); Dickason, *supra* n.72, at 151.

82 Lantigua, *supra* n.42, at 42.

83 *See id.* at 43.

84 *Id.* at 42–43.

Innocent's moderation contrasts with the stance taken by his influential student Hostiensis.[85] That canonist rejected all non-Christian *dominium*, believing that when Jesus Christ became incarnate, He received all the worldly power that previously belonged to infidels and gave it to the popes.[86] All infidels usurped Church authority (even if the Church should often tolerate this as a practical matter).[87]

Controversy between these two positions kept quiet for over a century due to "minimal" peaceful contact between the Church and non-Christian societies.[88] Then came the explosive fifteenth century, culminating in *Inter caetera*. First came debate over Lithuania, which was still pagan and contested by Poland and the Teutonic Knights.[89] To resolve their dispute, Antipope John XXIII (r. 1410–1415) called the Council of Constance (1414–1418).[90] There, the Knights rejected Lithuanians' *dominium* on account of their infidelity.[91] Council participants were unimpressed; one "dryly responded that all men were sinners."[92] The Council endorsed Innocent's position and rejected Hostiensis's.[93] But all was

85 *See* Mäkinen & Posti, *supra* n.72, at 175. For more regarding Hostiensis, see Kenneth Pennington, *Enrico da Susa (Cardinal Hostiensis) (ca. 1200–1271)*, in Condorelli & Domingo, *supra* n.67.

86 Muldoon, Popes, *supra* n.5, at 141; Michael Stogre S.J., That the World May Believe: The Development of Papal Social Thought on Aboriginal Rights 60–61 (1992).

87 *See* Stogre, *supra* n.86, at 61–62.

88 Muldoon, *Papal Responsibility*, *supra* n.63, at 173; *but see* Dickason, *supra* n.72, at 153–56 (noting commentaries in the interim); Mäkinen & Posti, *supra* n.72, at 176–80.

89 Muldoon, Popes, *supra* n.5, at 105.

90 *Id.* at 106. Regarding the Council, see Francis Oakley, The Conciliarist Tradition: Constitutionalism in the Catholic Church 1300–1870 pp. 20–22, 32–42 (2003).

91 Muldoon, Popes, *supra* n.5, at 107–09.

92 *Id.* at 111.

93 *See id.* at 119; Olivier Boulnois, *L'Usage et la Domination de Wyclif á John Locke*, 24 Przegląd Tomistyczny 531 (2018). Regarding the Polish response, see Michał Kowalski, *Stanisław of Skarbimierz (ca. 1360/65–1431) and Paweł Włodkowic (ca. 1370/73–1435/36)*, in Law and Christianity in Poland: The Legacy of the Great Jurists (Franciszek Longchamps de Bérier and Rafael Domingo eds., 2023). While the Council's decrees went without papal ratification, its judgment regarding infidel *dominium* remained influential. *See* Thomas Shahan, *Council of Constance*, in 4 Catholic Encyclopedia (1908), *available at* https://www.newadvent.org/cathen/04288a.htm.

Hostiensis's outlier status is sometimes overlooked. *See, e.g.*, Steven T. Newcomb, Pagans in the Promised Land: Decoding the Doctrine of Christian Discovery 108 (2008) [hereinafter "Pagans"] (arguing that Catholics saw infidels as lacking inherent rights); L.C. Green, *Claims to Territory in Colonial America*, in Green & Dickason, *supra* n.73, at 4 ("[F]rom the early part of the fourteenth century, it was generally accepted that the entire globe was the property of God and, as such, distributable by the Pope as His delegate on earth."). Note in this regard García Gallo's observation that the Portuguese never sought

not lost for the Knights and the many colonizers who would follow them. The new Pope Martin v (r. 1417–1431) confirmed the Knights' crusading privileges, and besides, Innocent's ideas could still support some conquests.[94]

The Guanche people of the Canary Islands endured the consequences of Innocent's vindication a few decades later. This episode began with a rare resounding victory for Indigenous rights. Pope Eugene IV (r. 1431–1447) learned that Christian slavers were abusing believer and infidel inhabitants alike.[95] This scandalized some Guanche out of their intention to be baptized, "thus offending the majesty of God, putting their souls in danger, and causing no little harm to the Christian religion."[96] Eugene ordered every slave freed and all expropriated property returned, on penalty of excommunication.[97]

The Portuguese were displeased, appealing in Innocentian terms for Eugene to allow colonization and calling his previous order "'the last obstacle' to civilizing and converting infidels."[98] Their request was "unprecedented" in seeking reversal of papal policy and in combining religious and civilizational rationales for colonization.[99] Eugene consulted with two canonists.[100] He then granted Portugal the exclusive right to conquer the Canaries in order to spread Christianity.[101]

---

papal authorization of their occupation of the Azores, Madeira, or Brazil, and Castile never sought it for its later occupation of the Canaries. *See* García Gallo, *supra* n.5, at 652–53.

94 *See* Lantigua, *supra* n.42, at 45.

95 *See* Muldoon, *Papal Responsibility*, *supra* n.63, at 177; Eugene IV, *Sicut Dudum* (Jan. 13, 1435), *reprinted in Appendix B to* Joel S. Panzer, The Popes and Slavery 75 (1996).

96 Eugene IV, *supra* n.95, at 76.

97 *See id.* at 77–78.

98 Lantigua, *supra* n.42, at 47.

99 *Id.*; *see also* Muldoon, *Papal Responsibility*, *supra* n.63, at 178 (describing the appeal as suggesting "a rudimentary conception of the 'White Man's Burden' more generally associated with the nineteenth century … interested not simply in uplifting the natives spiritually but in assisting them to develop their social and cultural level as well."). Europeans had long seen Africans and Muslims as socially inferior. *See* John Witte Jr., The Western Case for Monogamy Over Polygamy 159 (2015) ("Muslim polygamists, early polemicists wrote, were 'backward,' 'primitive,' 'barbaric,' 'lustful,' 'adulterous,' and 'incestuous.'"). Differences regarding sexual mores (real and perceived) also featured in Spanish depictions of Indigenous Americans. *See, e.g.*, Lantigua, *supra* n.42, at 62, 69.

100 *See* Lantigua, *supra* n.42, at 47; Muldoon, Popes, *supra* n.5, at 128. Scholar Luis Weckmann incorrectly thought that the Canarian intervention and *Inter caetera* presupposed papal lordship over all oceanic islands. *See* Luis Weckmann, Las Bulas Alejandrinas de 1493 y la Teoría Política del Papado Medieval: Estudio de la Supremacía Papal sobre Islas 1091–1493 pp. 259–60 (1949); *but see* García Gallo, *supra* n.5, at 663–69 (rebutting this convincingly).

101 *See* Lantigua, *supra* n.42, at 47.

Leading historian James Muldoon has described Eugene's conundrum: yield to the Portuguese demands or "stand by while European slave traders raided."[102] Eugene did not mention Guanche land rights, but may have seen his intervention as providing that conquest "would insure the spiritual and physical well-being of the native population" and avoid intra-Christian warfare.[103] Muldoon may be right that humanity motivated Eugene—after all, he had protected the Guanche. But he also had motives to change course. As Lind writes, the Portuguese may have convinced him that "little concern needed to be given to the Guanche interests in *dominium*, for depriving them of their earthly holdings was far outweighed by the spiritual rewards they could receive."[104] Indeed, even long before Innocent's acceptance of indirect coercion, Christians had approved of war to "clear[] the path of obstacles like idolatry that stood in the way of receiving the truth"; St. Augustine (354–430) identified this as one of the reasons why God let the pagan Roman Empire conquer the world.[105]

What was the practical effect of Eugene's decision? The Portuguese eventually ceded the Canaries to Castile, which conquered Tenerife in 1495–96. The new colonial governor gave the Guanche the choice of baptism, enslavement, or war; their chief committed ritual suicide.[106]

By then, popes frequently granted conquest rights. In 1341, Pope Benedict XII granted the Portuguese crusading privileges in Africa; in 1455, Pope Nicholas V sanctioned their ventures along the West African coast.[107] In doing so, both popes assumed that most Africans were Muslim enemies within the larger context of the ongoing religious wars.[108] Muslims still occupied Granada, and Africa-based Muslims had invaded Europe in each of the four preceding centuries.[109] Nicholas saw Portuguese incursion as a precursor to Christian

---

102 Muldoon, Popes, *supra* n.5, at 106; *see also* Muldoon, *Papal Responsibility*, *supra* n.63, at 180.

103 Muldoon, Popes, *supra* n.5, at 123; *see also id.* at 129–30 ("It must have been quite clear to the pope that European conquest of the Canary Islands, and of other lands occupied by infidels who did not pose a direct military threat to Christendom, would proceed with or without papal approval.").

104 Lind, *supra* n.39, at 15.

105 Lantigua, *supra* n.42, at 169.

106 *See id.* at 49–50.

107 *See* García Gallo, *supra* n.5, at 482–83, 672; Lind, *supra* n.39, at 15–16.

108 García Gallo, *supra* n.5, at 482–83; Muldoon, Americas, *supra* n.57, at 135; Muldoon, *Papal Responsibility*, *supra* n.63, at 181 (saying Nicholas did not distinguish among Africans).

109 See C. Raymond Beazley, *Prince Henry of Portugal and the African Crusade of the Fifteenth Century*, 16 Am. Hist. Rev. 11, 21–22 (1910).

reconquest of Iberia.[110] Besides, some Iberians saw themselves as recovering from Muslim conquerors the North Africa that had belonged to their Visigothic ancestors.[111] Portugal's "dream" of permanently occupying West Africa went unfulfilled, but Nicholas's intervention would prove another important precedent for *Inter caetera*.[112]

Returning to that bull, some scholars have interpreted it as a mere regulation of evangelization or Castilian-Portuguese relations.[113] Others, though, have treated it as dividing the world "into two open hunting grounds for the conquest of non-Christian peoples."[114] *Inter caetera*'s canonical precursors complicate that debate. Innocent recognized non-Christian *dominium*, Hostiensis disputed it, and both accepted war in aid of evangelization. Eugene accepted the Portuguese desire to conquer the Guanche in order to civilize and evangelize them. Nicholas sanctioned African wars as part of a broader struggle against Muslims. But Innocent tried to meet the Mongols with peace and qualified his acceptance of religious warfare, and Eugene defended all Guanche—regardless of religion—against Christian abuse.

At the time of *Inter caetera*, then, canon law held that the Papacy could grant with one hand the right to conquer and, with the other, limit its exercise. What

---

110 *See id.* Beazley also discusses Christian rumors that a mighty African Christian king known as "Prester John" would soon join in the wars against Muslims. *See id.* at 18, 22.

111 See José Luis Egío & Christiane Birr, *Alonso de Cartagena y Juan López de Palacios Rubios. Dilemas Suscitados por las Primeras Conquistas Atlánticas en Dos Juristas Salmantinos (1436–1512)*, 20 Azafea: Revista Filosófica 9, 23 (2018) ("[S]e hacen pasar como episodios de un plan consciente destinado a restaurar el dominio ejercido por los reyes hispanos en el norte de África en la época de mayor dilatación territorial del reino visigodo. ... [Alonso de] Cartagena se concentra en probar la existencia de una usurpación histórica y denuncia la ausencia de un 'título justo' en el dominio ejercido por los infieles ...." ["These can be considered episodes of a conscious plan destined to restore the lordship exercised by the Hispanic kings in North Africa in the age of the Visigothic kingdom's greatest territorial reach ... [Alonso de] Cartagena [c.1385–1486] concentrates on proving the existence of a historic usurpation and denounces the absence of a 'just title' in the dominion exercised by the infidels ...."]).

112 *See* Beazley, *supra* n.109, at 22.

113 *See* Muldoon, *Colonial Charters*, *supra* n.50, at 380; Muldoon, Popes, *supra* n.5, at 137; Muldoon, *Papal Responsibility*, *supra* n.63, at 169; García Gallo, *supra* n.5, at 609–10.

114 Scott, *supra* n.5, at 348; *see also* Lind, *supra* n.39, at 17 ("By virtue of the bulls ... Portugal and Spain thus could explore, subdue, and assert dominion over all non-Christian peoples and lands worldwide, on behalf of and in the name of Christendom."); *cf.* José Luis Egío & Christiane Birr, *Before Vitoria: Expansion into Heathen, Empty, or Disputed Lands in Late-Mediaeval Salamanca Writings and Early 16th-Century Juridical Treatises*, in Tellkamp, *supra* n.72 [hereinafter "*Before Vitoria*"] (explaining that Bernardino López de Carvajal, the Spaniard who negotiated *Inter caetera*, followed Hostiensis's opinion regarding infidel *dominium*; however, Egío and Birr ultimately deem the bull to have been mere "corroboration and endorsement").

did Alexander mean to do with his bull? Perhaps both: sanction Castilian conquest, but with moral regulation for Indigenous welfare.[115] The tension inherent in trying to do so is obvious. But nothing requires that principles translate coherently in practice, especially when consequences remain veiled in the future. Which was certainly the case in 1493.

3.2 *History: Columbus's Discovery of the West Indies*

The shroud has now been torn. We know that the Spanish colonized massive parts of two continents, then pressed on to a third. Tens of millions of people became their subjects. Millions perished from European-borne war and disease.

None of this was foreseeable in 1492 when Columbus set sail, nor the following year when Alexander issued *Inter caetera*. A decade earlier, Spain and Portugal thought they had resolved their dispute over who would rule the few islands in the vast sea surrounding Eurasia. While Columbus was prepared to claim a few outposts along the route to the Far East, he did not set sail ready to conquer a whole world of unknown people. At the time of *Inter caetera*, Europeans "still credited medieval legends of enchanted kingdoms … inhabited by Amazons, giants, and even more exotic life forms such as hydras, griffins, and dragons who guarded hoards of precious things."[116] Only the slow apprehension of the actual New World that Columbus had encountered would bring Europeans to rethink canon-law precedents. *Inter caetera*'s **historical context**—the knowledge gap that made the bull so momentous in hindsight—also has relevance to what Alexander may have meant by it.

In 1479, a mere thirteen years before Columbus's *Niña*, *Pinta*, and *Santa Maria* set sail, Castile and Portugal negotiated the Treaty of Alcaçovas (confirmed in 1481 by Pope Sixtus IV).[117] It formalized what naval combat had already decided: the Portuguese would rule the then-discovered Atlantic islands, including the Azores, Madeiras, and Cabo Verde, and any other lands

115 *See* García Gallo, *supra* n.5, at 475 (noting that attempts to reconstruct *Inter caetera's* original meaning end in speculation); Lantigua, *supra* n.42, at 48 ("[C]onquest and evangelization were compatible, mutually supportive practices."); Friedrich August Freiherr von der Heydte, *Discovery, Symbolic Annexation and Virtual Effectiveness in International Law*, 29 Am. J. Int'l L. 448, 451–52 (1935) ("The Pope awarded his donations only in order to further the conversion of the inhabitants of the discovered territories by means of occupation by Spain and Portugal; he was interested, therefore, in discoveries only as far as they led to a thorough occupation.'" (quoting Walter Fuglsang, Der Amerikanisch-Holländische Streit um die Insel Palmas vor dem Ständigen Schiedshof im Haag 83 (1931))). Von der Heydte was a Nazi military officer. *See* Maj. Johann Hindert, *German Views of Irregular Warfare* at 7–8 (June 2015) (unpub. M.S. thesis, Nav. Postgrad. Sch. [U.S.]), *available at* https://apps.dtic.mil/sti/pdfs/ADA632373.pdf.

116 Lyle N. McAlister, Spain and Portugal in the New World, 1492–1700 p. 89 (1984).

117 *See* Scott, *supra* n.5, at 350.

discovered in the open seas.[118] No one thought at that point that unknown continents lay out there.[119] The Alcaçovas settlement was backed by a solemn invocation that violators would "incur the wrath of Almighty God and of the blessed apostles Peter and Paul."[120]

But then, Ferdinand sent Columbus off into the forbidden western zone.[121] Indeed, the returning Columbus put in at the Azores during a storm and was arrested before the Portuguese realized he was not coming from Africa (upon seeing the non-African natives he brought back with him); when he proceeded on to Lisbon, the possibility of killing him for breaking the treaty was apparently considered.[122] Only after this did Ferdinand secure a new papal document. Doing so proved easy, perhaps because Alexander (birth name Rodrigo Lanzol y Borja—in Italian, Borgia) was a native Spaniard and owed Ferdinand for appointing *Alexander's teenage son* archbishop of Valencia.[123] Or maybe it was because Alexander was indeed an afterthought to power politics.[124]

---

118 *Id.* The first three were truly uninhabited when Europeans arrived. *See* Muldoon, *Colonial Charters*, *supra* n.50, at 365 n.37.

119 *See id.*; Lind, *supra* n.39, at 19 ("Columbus' voyages to the West Indies, along with other European maritime adventures, such as Vasco da Gama's discovery of a sea route to India in 1498 and Ferdinand Magellan's circumnavigation of the earth from 1519 to 1522, left Europeans convinced that there was substantial land unknown to them lying beyond their continent.").

120 Sixtus IV, *The Bull* Aeterni Regis (June 21, 1481), *reprinted in* Davenport, *supra* n.5, at 55 (ratifying the treaty); id. at 52 (the Latin); see also Treaty of Alcacovas, Sept. 4, 1479, Castile-Port. (Frances Gardiner Davenport trans., 1917), *available at* https://avalon.law.yale.edu/15th_century/sppoo1.asp.

121 *See* Scott, *supra* n.5, at 350. Generously, perhaps Ferdinand only meant to creatively skirt the treaty. See the discussions above and below on effective occupation as a debated prerequisite to territorial rights.

122 *See* Stogre, *supra* n.86, at 69–70.

123 *See* Scott, *supra* n.5, at 351; Alexander Lee, *Were the Borgias Really So Bad?*, Hist. Today, Oct. 1, 2013, https://www.historytoday.com/history-matters/were-borgias-really-so-bad (doubting the occurrence of the infamous Banquet of Chestnuts orgy, but calling Alexander "lusty and sexually adventurous"); *Borgia Apartment*, Musei Vaticani, https://www.museivaticani.va/content/museivaticani/en/collezioni/musei/appartamento-borgia/appartamento-borgia.html ("[His] apartment was abandoned by Julius II (1503–1513), who did not wish to be surrounded by the memory of his despised predecessor ...."). The son proved no saintlier. As a cardinal, Cesare Borgia (*c.*1475/76–1507) was best known for "his hunting parties, his amorous liaisons, and his magnificent clothes"; then, as a layman, his ruthlessness and cunning made him Niccolò Machiavelli's model prince. Michael Edward Mallett, *Cesare Borgia*, Britannica, https://www.britannica.com/biography/Cesare-Borgia.

124 *See* Lantigua, *supra* n.42, at 56 ("[T]he Pope was a *post facto* formal notary ...."); *but see* Creighton, *supra* n.50, at 170, 172 (noting Isabella and Ferdinand's eagerness to secure papal approval in order to foreclose Portuguese claims).

What about Columbus himself? Did he set out in hopes of conquering the world, or with something tamer in mind? The evidence is mixed.[125] Lantigua finds Columbus's aim "incandescent: to ascertain the manner of bringing about infidel conversion to the Christian faith," including "through political control."[126] He relies on Columbus's journal, including an entry saying Columbus would not pass any island "without taking possession of it."[127] Columbus did in fact immediately claim possession of the first island he reached.[128] He also wrote Isabella and Ferdinand that the Indies were "as much your own as Castile" and they would soon be able to "command" the natives "to do what you wish."[129] Isabella also initially agreed with Columbus that the Caribs should be enslaved, partly (echoing Innocent) to ease "instruction in the faith and incorporation into Christendom."[130]

But this determination to dominate came about only after Columbus had observed Indians and deemed them primitive.[131] No one had anticipated finding such people.[132] There is evidence that when Columbus first departed, neither he nor his royal patrons thought he had a conquering mandate, or even an evangelizing one. In his journal, he described his mission as "to go to the mainland and to the city of Quisay and to present Your Highnesses' letters to

125 *See* Gustavo Gutiérrez, Las Casas: In Search of the Poor of Jesus Christ 472–73 (Robert R. Barr trans., 1993) (noting modern scholarship about the intertwining of religious mission with secular adventurism). Fr. Gutiérrez, a Peruvian Dominican, is the father of "liberation theology." *See generally* Gustavo Gutiérrez, A Theology of Liberation: History, Politics, and Salvation (rev'd ed., Orbis Books 1988) (1971); Congregation for the Doctrine of the Faith, *Instruction on Certain Aspects of the 'Theology of Liberation'* (Aug. 6, 1984), *available at* https://www.ewtn.com/catholicism/library/instruction-on-certain-aspects-of-the-theology-of-liberation-2097.

126 Lantigua, *supra* n.42, at 53.

127 *Id.*

128 *See* Bartolomé de Las Casas and the Defense of Amerindian Rights: A Brief History with Documents 33 (Lawrence A. Clayton & David M. Lantigua eds., 2020).

129 Lantigua, *supra* n.42, at 55.

130 *Id.* at 61.

131 *See id.* at 55–56; Clayton & Lantigua, *supra* n.128, at 33–34 (quoting Columbus's immediate impressions: "[I]t seemed to me that they were a people very poor in everything. All of them go around as naked as their mothers bore them .... They do not carry arms nor are they acquainted with them .... They have no iron.").

132 Muldoon, Americas, *supra* n.57, at 23 ("What [Columbus] found was a new, or at least an unexpected and previously unknown, land that stood between him and the land of the Khan. This was a land inhabited by people who had not developed trade, government, and the other elements of civil society."); García Gallo, *supra* n.5, at 478 ("Las bulas no se ocupan para nada de América. En 1493 nadie sabe que existe el continente .... ["The bulls did not concern America at all. In 1493, no one knew that the continent exists"]").

the Grand Khan, and to beg a reply and to come home with it."[133] Historian Wilcomb E. Washburn split the difference and found it highly unlikely that Columbus or any other European "expected to sail to Asiatic shores and immediately 'take over,'" even though they did think they would "take possession of minor offshore islands."[134] His evidence: Vasco da Gama, who made it to (the real) India, "came with cautious respect and regard for the diplomatic niceties."[135] And Columbus set out with an interpreter of Semitic languages, "a Latin passport, Latin letter of credence from Ferdinand and Isabella, and a royal gift."[136] Muldoon summarizes:

> Generally speaking, Europeans only claimed the right to acquire those territories that were vacant or were occupied by people who lived at a primitive level. The debate about the right to acquire infidel societies did not include consideration of more developed societies such as China and Japan. The chief interest of Europeans in these societies was trade, not their conquest and subordination. Christian Europeans had long traded with Muslim societies, and there was no general ecclesiastical prohibition against trading with infidels. Consequently, there was no reason to attempt the conquest of those societies, an activity, even if it could have succeeded, which would have been counterproductive.[137]

This peaceful way of seeing non-Christians was still new. Fifteenth-century Europe was only just becoming "uncomfortably aware that the 'world' was now composed of a multiplicity of cultures and of independent states, some of which, in particular the Ottoman ... and the Chinese, were almost as large in territorial extension, and quite as sophisticated, as any European polity."[138] In this context, Columbus's first journey was hardly the making of a worldwide crusade, even if many Christians did believe on some abstract—perhaps even eschatological—level that "one day all the lands of the earth would be placed under Christian sovereignty and dominion" (as indeed, many still believe today).[139]

---

133 *Quoted in* Tzvetan Todorov, The Conquest of America: The Question of the Other 10 (Richard Howard trans., 1984).

134 Wilcomb E. Washburn, *The Meaning of "Discovery" in the Fifteenth and Sixteenth Centuries*, 68 Am. Hist. Rev. 1, 8 (1962).

135 *Id.*

136 *Id.* at 8–9.

137 Muldoon, Americas, *supra* n.57, at 23.

138 Pagden, Lords, *supra* n.44, at 38.

139 Newcomb, *Evidence*, *supra* n.19, at 335; *see also* Newcomb, Pagans, *supra* n.93, at 31 (overstating his case that *Inter caetera* presupposes that "the conqueror is being most virtuous, morally sound, and obedient to God when he uses the tools of coercion, terror, fear, and

Additionally, Columbus's initial commission "did not make any claim that the Spanish monarchs in any way owned or had a right to seize the as yet undiscovered lands" nor "suggest that Columbus would conquer territory."[140] Its reference to land acquisitions meant trade outposts and harbors.[141] Nothing indicated that Columbus was to start large-scale colonization, there was no reference to any immediate religious mission, and although he was to establish a basis for future evangelization (and indeed gave natives rudimentary instruction in Christianity), his crew had no priests.[142] He did hold generous mineral, resource, and monetary rights.[143] But his only political authority, Muldoon writes, "clearly referred to jurisdiction over subjects of the Spanish monarchs living in [newly claimed] lands or those indigenous people who submitted to Spanish jurisdiction."[144] While Columbus did have a *personal* religious mission, it was financing a new crusade to retake Jerusalem—not converting islanders. Meanwhile, Isabella and Ferdinand "reserved the right to employ the potential profit of the undertaking for other purposes" (and in fact did so).[145] Nothing suggests that Columbus set off to become the infidel world's *conquistador*. Indeed, on a subsequent voyage in June 1494, his crew still expressed confidence "that in not too many leagues further on there 'must be' highly cultivated people" of the sort they had set out to meet.[146]

Alexander issued *Inter caetera* even before this, with no idea what Columbus had actually discovered. As far as both men understood, Columbus had found a

---

dread to fulfill 'God's will' by conquering and subduing new lands and new peoples not yet conquered."); Washburn, *supra* n.134, at 18 ("[Columbus] signed [a 1502] letter ... with the title 'The Great Admiral of the Ocean Sea, and Viceroy and Governor of the Islands and Mainland of Asia and the Indies belonging to the King and Queen, my sovereigns, and their Captain-General of the Sea, and a member of their Council.' ... [This] demonstrates Columbus' conception of the theoretical location of Asia combined with his knowledge of Spain's actual power over the lands he discovered. It is not proof of his assumption or intention, before the voyage, to take over the government of the 'Asia' known to fifteenth-century Europe.").

140 Muldoon, *Colonial Charters*, *supra* n.50, at 363; *Capitulaciones de Sante Fe*, *reprinted in* La Conquista del Nuevo Mundo: Textos y Documentos de la Aventura Americana 71–74 (Mercedes Serna ed., 2012).

141 *See* Muldoon, *Colonial Charters*, *supra* n.50, at 363.

142 *See id.*; *see generally Capitulaciones de Sante Fe*, *supra* n.140; García Gallo, *supra* n.5, at 638–44.

143 *See* Scott, *supra* n.5, at 350.

144 Muldoon, *Colonial Charters*, *supra* n.50, at 363.

145 Todorov, *supra* n.133, at 11; *see also* Beazley, *supra* n.109, at 23 ("[W]hen he made [his will] (on February 22, 1498) ... Columbus still hoped for better things; but, in the last resort, if Castile and Aragon were still deaf to the cause of the Holy City, then he lays it upon his heir to perform this conquest, alone if need be, all if it might be, and if not all, then whatever part he could.").

146 Washburn, *supra* n.134, at 9.

few islands populated by primitive people. Alexander would have found these circumstances familiar in light of the Canarian and African precedents.[147] So would the Castilians, who would have seen the situation as more suited to civilization through colonization than to diplomatic dealing. This helps explain why the royals turned to the Papacy, just as Portugal had done in the earlier cases.[148] In turn, *Inter caetera* cast Indians in much the same light as the Portuguese had the Guanche: "a primitive but peace-loving people who seemed quite willing to accept the Christian faith."[149] In another parallel, a pope was addressing

147 *See* José Luis Egío García, *Matías De Paz and the Introduction of Thomism in the* Asuntos de Indias*: A Conceptual Revolution*, 26 Rechstgeschichte/L. Hist. 236, 237 (2018) ("[T]he first theological and juridical discussions about the status of those 'infidel' peoples ... appear to be, in fact, a clear and direct continuation of the Late Middle Ages approach ...."); Weckmann, *supra* n.100, at 31 ("Se olvida que la cancillería papal es una de las instituciones más metódicas y rutinarias de Europa y que la redacción de bulas papales sigue, dentro de lo factible, y preferentemente, rutas ya trazadas y moldes tradicionales tomados de previos documentos. ... [D]e haberse descubierto el Nuevo Mundo ... hubiera seguido cronológicamente al de las islas portuguesas del África .... ["It has been forgotten that the papal chancery is one of the most methodical and routinized institutions in Europe and that the drafting of papal bulls follows, to the extent possible, and preferentially, routes already traced and traditional molds taken from previous documents ... [T]he New World's discovery ... would have followed chronologically that of the Portuguese islands of Africa"]"); García Gallo, *supra* n.5, at 470 (*citing* Pedro de Leturia, Las Grandes Bulas Misionales de Alejandro VI, 1493 pp. 209–51 (1930), in noting connections between *Inter caetera* and Portugal's African expeditions). Stogre reasonably speculates that the Guanche's then-recent subjugation by Castile would have inspired Alexander to try to limit abuses. *See* Stogre, *supra* n.86, at 70–71; *see also* Muldoon, Popes, *supra* n.5, at 137; *see also id.* at 138 ("Columbus' description of the people he met as primitive and simple would encourage papal support for the conquest in order to protect these simple people from exploitation by wicked Europeans, just as Eugenius IV had accepted the Portuguese claim that they would protect the Canarians."); Muldoon, *Papal Responsibility*, *supra* n.63, at 182 ("[T]he granting of the Americas to the Castilians was based on the argument that the natives require protection and that the pope, in the absence of any other authority ... was required by the nature of his vicariate of Christ to provide the protection."). But García Gallo also reasonably speculates that Indigenous peoples were simply not a conscious concern for most of the papal bulls sanctioning domination. *See* García Gallo, *supra* n.5, at 611–12.

148 *See* Muldoon, Americas, *supra* n.57, at 23.

149 *See Inter caetera*, *supra* n.5, at 76 ("... Columbus ... discovered certain very remote islands and even mainlands that hitherto had not been discovered by others; wherein dwell very many peoples living in peace, and, as reported, going unclothed, and not eating flesh. Moreover, as your aforesaid envoys are of opinion, these very peoples living in the said islands and countries believe in one God, the Creator in heaven, and seem sufficiently disposed to embrace the Catholic faith and be trained in good morals. And it is hoped that, were they instructed, the name of the Savior, our Lord Jesus Christ, would easily be introduced ....").

overseas developments that were already under way.[150] *Inter caetera* may have been a mere formality.

But Columbus himself also leaves early evidence of its significance for conquest. Writing to the Castilian monarchs from Central America, he said that the bull left him "so persuaded of the legitimacy of Spain's title to the Indies that he considered Their Majesties 'just as much political lords of this land as of Jerez or Toledo'" back in Spain.[151] Mere puffery? Perhaps. Recall his pre-*Inter caetera* flattery that the West Indies were "as much your own as Castile."[152] But his letter foretold the bull's role in the Spanish Empire. By 1503, it featured in royal deliberations.[153] Isabella's last will of 1504 cited it in incorporating the West Indies into her realms.[154]

At that point, though, no one knew exactly what Columbus had found. A mere fifteen years before, Spain and Portugal had been squabbling over a few Atlantic islands. Columbus figured he could pass by them, plant a few flags, and show up at the khanate court bearing gifts. He was surprised to find Indigenous Caribbean peoples along the way. But in 1493, the magnitude of his discovery was still a matter more of myth than of meticulous study. Explorers still

---

150 Muldoon, Popes, *supra* n.5, at 138.

151 *Quoted in* Lewis Hanke, The Spanish Struggle for Justice in the Conquest of America 25 (1949) [hereinafter "Struggle"].

152 Lantigua, *supra* n.42, at 55.

153 *See* Hanke, Struggle, *supra* n.151, at 174 ("[Ferdinand] indignantly cited an earlier discussion in 1503, at which it was unanimously agreed that the papal donation provided ample justification [for colonization] ….").

154 *See* Testamento y Codicilo de la Reina Isabel la Católica: 12 de octubre y 23 de noviembre de 1504 p. 33 (Ministerio de Educación y Ciencia (Esp.) 2013) (1504)) [hereinafter Testamento] ("[L]as Islas e Tierra Firme del Mar Oçeano … han de quedar incorporados en estos mis reynos de Castilla e Leon, segund que en la bulla apostolica a nos sobrella conçedida se contiene …." ["The Islands and Firm Land of the Ocean Sea … must remain incorporated in my realms of Castile and Leon, as the apostolic bull conceded to us provides"]). In time, overseas possessions became "separate kingdoms—the *reinos de Indias* ["Indian realms"]—governed by a separate body of legislation (codified in 1680) and administered by a royal council." Pagden, *European Background, supra* n.51, at 1; *see also* Barrientos, *supra* n.5, at 88–93 (describing the process of incorporation).

Steven T. Newcomb concludes that Isabella's will regards Indigenous land title as "subject to the overriding dominion of the Crown," relying on a translation of the codicil saying the royals sought *Inter caetera* to "gain and *takeover* their [the Indians'] homeland and convert them to our holy Catholic faith." *Evidence, supra* n.19, at 316 n.82 (quoting W. Eugene Shiels, King and Church: The Rise and Fall of the Patronato Real 99 (1961) (emphasis added)). The Castilian reads: "procurar de ynduzir e traer los pueblos [de las Yslas e Tierra Firme del Mar Oçeano] e les convertir a nuestra santa fe catholica." Testamento at 42. I would render the key language more softly as "to try to induce and bring the peoples [of the Islands and Mainland of the Ocean] and convert them to our holy Catholic faith." Thanks to Rafael Domingo for his suggestions.

believed that somewhere out there "lay El Dorado, Gran Quivira, the Seven Cities of Cíbola, and the formidable Nation of the Amazons."[155] In light of his historical context, Alexander simply could not have grasped the significance of the bull he wrote. Did he mean to give Castile the whole Indigenous world? No. He thought he was addressing only a few Caribbean islands. Not China or India. Certainly not a whole hemisphere.

But that does not answer the question of whether Alexander meant for *Inter caetera* to give *part* of the world away through conquest. Did he want merely to guide Castile's ventures, or to legitimize them? The historical context points in both directions. The fact that the bull was issued only after the invasion had begun is relevant, of course. But so are the Canarian and African precedents. In light of them, Alexander surely knew that his bull would bless some conquest. What is more, he had geopolitical reasons to do so.

3.3 *Geopolitics: Conflict between Christendom and Islam*

Inter caetera did not emerge out of a vacuum. Wars had raged for centuries between Muslim powers and Christendom. These drastically affected trade routes between Europe and Asia. But Spain, recently reconquered by Christians, carried hopes for a revitalized Christian empire. Alongside its rise came a struggle by popes to reclaim political relevance. In this **geopolitical context**, Alexander had much to gain by positioning the Church as an ally of Castilian colonization.

The conflict between the Christian and Islamic worlds helped define the fifteenth century. Muslims continued to rule Granada until 1492.[156] The Ottoman Turks had conquered Constantinople in 1453, controlled Europe-Asia trade routes, and in 1529, even besieged Vienna.[157] The Papacy saw colonization as a way to sway the balance of power back toward Christendom. Exploration could help Christians regain control over Asian commerce, but popes also wanted to expand European sovereignty.[158] I have already mentioned their vision of the Portuguese occupying West Africa.[159] Christians held fast to legends that somewhere in that continent there reigned a powerful Christian king named Prester John who would fight Islam.[160] Muldoon writes that Pope Nicholas ultimately wanted Portuguese victories to unite "Latin Christians with those

155 McAlister, *supra* n.116, at 455.

156 *See* Beazley, *supra* n.109, at 21–22.

157 *See* Anthony F.C. Wallace et al., *How to Buy a Continent: The Protocol of Indian Treaties as Developed by Benjamin Franklin and Other Members of the American Philosophical Society*, 159 Proceedings Am. Phil. Soc'y 251, 264 (2015).

158 *See id.*

159 *See* Beazley, *supra* n.109, at 21–22.

160 *See id.* at 18, 22.

Christians who lived beyond the Moslem world. Then the Moslems would be crushed as in a vise by the two branches of the one Church."[161]

Spain carried such hopes, too, especially once Charles V (King of Spain from 1516, Holy Roman Emperor 1519–1556) and his Habsburg relatives dynastically linked it with Naples, Milan, and the Holy Roman Empire.[162] Add Spanish victory over Iberian Muslim rulers, national religious fervor after this *Reconquista*, and the election as pope of Adrian VI (r. 1522–1523)—a former Castilian regent—and Spain looked like Rome reincarnate, ready to reorder the world for the Church.[163]

In the same era, the popes wanted to reestablish their own leading role as well. The Papacy had suffered during both its exile from Rome into Avignon (1309–1377) and the Western Schism (1378–1417), when rivals asserted claims to the papal chair.[164] The popes tried to recover prominence in international affairs by intervening in the disputes over Lithuania, the Canaries, and the African mainland.[165]

Of course, European powers often acted first and sought Vatican approval later.[166] And even when popes acted, their decisions could be quickly

161 *See* Muldoon, Popes, *supra* n.5, at 134–35.

162 Pagden, Lords, supra n.44, at 41; see also Yuri Mantilla, *The Implementation of the Right to Self-Determination of Aymara and Quechua Indigenous Peoples: An International Normative Response to the Spanish Conquest of Tawantinsuyu*, 36 Emory Int'l L. Rev. 287, 303 (2022) [hereinafter "Tawantinsuyu"]. "Tawantinsuyu" refers to the Incan realms. *See id.* at 299.

163 *See* Pagden, Lords, *supra* n.44, at 43; James Loughlin, *Pope Adrian VI*, 1 Catholic Encyclopedia (1907), *available at* https://www.newadvent.org/cathen/01159b.htm; David A. Lupher, Romans in a New World: Classical Models in Sixteenth-Century Spanish America (2003).

164 Muldoon, Popes, *supra* n.5, at 105–06; *see also* O'Brien, *supra* n.69, at 28–29 ("When Pius II [r. 1458–1464] came to the throne, the papacy's once-extensive powers over the universal church now lay largely in the hands of secular princes. These rulers prohibited papal taxation in their territories or collected those taxes themselves; they limited or banned judicial appeals to Rome; they curbed or outlawed annates; and they enjoyed substantial control over provisions to benefices and appointments."); *id.* at 31 (describing popes' difficulties in recruiting sovereigns for crusades); *id.* at 40–41 (noting prominent critiques of papal temporal power); Elizabeth McCahill, Reviving the Eternal City: Rome and the Papal Court 1420–1447 p. 153 (2013) ("[M]any secular rulers ... sought to manipulate the crisis ... in order to increase the independence of their national churches."); Oakley, *supra* n.90, at 20–22, 32–51.

165 *See* Muldoon, Popes, *supra* n.5, at 105–06.

166 *See id.* at 136 ("The course of European conquest in the Atlantic was similar to that of the conquest and Christianization of Lithuania. ... What was at stake was the final organization of the conquest. At the same time, the popes continued to act as if their court could resolve disputes between Christian rulers."); Muldoon, *Papal Responsibility*, *supra* n.63, at 183–84 ("With the existence of peace between [Castile and Portugal] there was no longer any possibility of the pope being able to influence the colonial administrative policies of

dismissed: for instance, *Inter caetera*'s line between Castile and Portugal was almost immediately shifted by the Treaty of Tordesillas, a precedent repeated half a century later in the Pacific.[167] Still, through *Inter caetera* and other documents, the popes "legalized, recognized, [and] sanctioned *ex post facto* territorial sovereignty which already existed in fact, or they gave assent, and thereby legal sanction *ex ante* to an intended occupancy, to a condition anticipated in the future."[168]

In this context, Alexander was not a mere victim of imperial happenstance. Many years of war and lost trade had made Europeans eager to recover influence, and the Spanish offered much promise. For their part, previous popes did not want to simply keep watch over the shifting tides of power: they wanted to exert force over them.

A bull like *Inter caetera* was one way of exercising influence. Alexander's effort was symbolic, but "[i]sn't the symbolic the domain *par excellence* of religion?"[169] Law symbolically affords "an intelligibility for governing common life and the relations between peoples," while theology symbolically "navigates between worldview and interpretation of religious sources."[170] Neither always leads political developments. But Alexander and the fifteenth-century popes, positioning themselves as symbolic evaluators and interpreters of geopolitics—that is, acting as lawyers and theologians—did retake a central role in European life. To call *Inter caetera* the product of Spanish designs only

one kingdom by threatening to withdraw papal approval for conquest ...."); Scott, *supra* n.5, at 348 (rejecting the idea that *Inter caetera* "played some significant part in history, that it was obeyed by monarchs and therefore affected the course of events").

167 *See id.* at 139; José Antonio Cervera, The School of Salamanca at the End of the Known World in the 16th Century: Martín de Rada, Domingo de Salazar and Juan Cobo in the Philippines, 1565–1594 at 8 (School of Salamanca Working Paper Series 2019-02), *available at* https://publikationen.ub.uni-frankfurt.de/opus4/frontdoor/deliver/index/docId/46523/file/SvSal_WP_2019-02.pdf; *cf.* Tamar Herzog, Frontiers of Possession: Spain and Portugal in Europe and the Americas 17–18 (2015) (describing bilateral resolution of an early dispute over the Moluccas); Scott, *supra* n.5, at 348 ("... Charles V sent an expedition to the Philippines two years after he had sold all claim to the islands to the Portuguese crown, and when his son Philip actually occupied the archipelago, he did so not because any pope gave him permission but because the Portuguese could not prevent it.").

168 Von der Heydte, *supra* n.115, at 451–52.

169 Roussel, *supra* n.28, at 3, 22 ("Le symbolique n'est-il pas le domaine par excellence de la religion?"). Eugene in particular understood the Papacy's symbolic power and bolstered it through acts like the Canarian intervention. *See* McCahill, *supra* n.164, at 140 ("Analysis of his use of ceremony (like analysis of his plans for religious reform) suggests ... that Eugenius thought carefully about how to surmount the challenges he faced. ... By the end of his reign, Eugenius regained the political power that he had enacted ....").

170 Roussell, *supra* n.28, at 24 ("[L]e droit ... donne une intelligibilité pour régir la vie commune et les relations entre les peuples, la théologie navigue entre vision du monde et interprétation des sources religieuses.").

is to overlook this. By symbolically giving Castile new power, Alexander garnered some for himself and the Church as well.

3.4 *Evaluating* Inter caetera *in Its Contexts: Alexander's Ambiguities*

Did Alexander mean to give Castile a global empire? Contextual evidence cuts both ways. **Canon law** empowered him to both authorize conquests and limit how they were conducted. Which purpose was primary in *Inter caetera*? Maybe neither. Alexander may have wanted to sanction expansion into non-Christian islands while also keeping it from becoming pure exploitation. **History** certainly gives some reason to doubt the world-conquest narrative: Alexander thought his bull was addressing a few islands and their inhabitants, not vast civilized continents. However, from the Canarian and African episodes, he also knew that his words would be used to forcefully subject peoples to foreign rule. Meanwhile, **geopolitics** pushed Alexander toward supporting this as a way to counter Islamic gains and symbolically connect the Church to rising Spanish power.

Alexander did not think *Inter caetera* would inaugurate worldwide conquest, and he may have even meant for the bull to protect Indigenous peoples from the war that was already underway. But he also meant to give Isabella and Ferdinand a world to govern for the benefit of Indigenous peoples, Europeans, and the Church. It just turned out to be far larger and more populous than anyone imagined. So did Spanish debates about *Inter caetera*.

4 *Inter caetera* Interpreted: Debate across the Atlantic

Over the next 150 years, Spaniards in the home country and the colonies argued intensely about the meaning of *Inter caetera*. The earliest debates concerned what it required of Spaniards as they imposed their rule. A more fundamental question followed: was *Inter caetera* even legitimate? Vitoria said no and proposed alternative justifications for empire founded in natural law. But even after him, others would laud the bull as important authority. The significance of Alexander's words is evidenced by the early, middle, and late Spanish disputes over how they should be **interpreted**.

4.1 *Early Reception: Conquest, Protest, and Rules*

Inter caetera was the subject of much discussion in the early decades of colonization. Spaniards initially took the bull as a mandate to conquer. But Dominicans (members of a preaching order) sent on mission to Hispaniola mightily protested Indigenous enslavement and exploitation. In response, a Spanish theologian developed canon law to recognize some Indigenous rights, while a jurist adapted *Inter caetera* into an ultimatum for native peoples: submit or be conquered. During this period the bull, like its precedents, served as a basis for conquest and a limit on it.

4.1.1 First Invasions (1490s–Early 1500s): *Inter caetera* as Sanction

The Spanish initially understood *Inter caetera* as a straightforward justification for war. While Lantigua may be right that the Spanish understood it to primarily assign a "divine right ... to bring the Christian faith to the infidels across the Atlantic,"[171] Pekka Hämäläinen is correct that they equated this with "territorial control through social control."[172] Legal historian (and, speaking of seizing territory in wars of aggression, Nazi officer) Friedrich August Freiherr von der Heydte even suggested that all papal grants of territory became fully effective only upon occupation.[173] Christiane Birr summarizes the similar position of Spanish jurist Juan López de Palacios Rubios (1450–1524) (he is discussed more in Part 4.1.4 below) that "an occupying army should at the very least take and hold the main towns and localities (including the capture of fortified locations). In other words, he who cannot hold the capital, the *locus principalis*, has not conquered the island at all" and so has not actualized any rights.[174]

Ferdinand may have held this understanding as well. At the very least, in 1510, he went so far as to ask an ambassador to procure a new bull "allowing him to make war and conquer any territory dominated by infidels."[175] Pope Clement VII (r. 1523–1534) agreed to this in a limited sense: in a letter to Charles V, he wrote of the Americas: "We trust that ... you will compel and with all zeal

171 Lantigua, *supra* n.42, at 52.

172 Pekka Hämäläinen, *The Shapes of Power: Indians, Europeans, and North American Worlds from the Seventeenth to the Nineteenth Century*, in Contested Spaces of Early America 40 (Juliana Barr et al. eds., 2017).

173 *See* note 115 *supra*; von der Heydte, *supra* n.115, at 452, 457–58; Barrientos, *supra* n.5, at 20–26 (discussing occupation-based theories of civil jurist Bartolus of Saxoferrato (1313/14–1357)).

174 Christiane Birr, Dominium *in the Indies. Juan López de Palacios Rubios'* Libellus de insulis oceanis quas vulgus indias appelat (*1512–1516*), 26 Rechtsgeschichte/L. Hist. 264, 279 (2018).

175 *See* García, *supra* n.147, at 245; *see also* Miller, *Chile*, *supra* n.50, at 853–56, 868 (observing Spanish speed in marking new discoveries and effectively occupying them in order to preempt challenges, but also observing that Spain claimed territories its people had never even seen); Robert A. Williams Jr., The American Indian in Western Legal Thought: The Discourses of Conquest 204 (1990) (noting Spain's assertion of claims over Virginia in the time of King James I (r. England 1603–1625), despite its distance from any Spanish settlements).

cause the barbarian nations to come to the knowledge of God ... not only by edicts and admonitions, but also by force and arms, if needful."[176]

Inter caetera was not understood only as a spiritual mandate: for many, conquering souls and conquering societies went hand-in-hand.[177] Still, the connection between these two goals was (at most) implicit in the bull, and the occupation theory was never universally held.[178] That left room for debate about Alexander's intended meaning. Within a few years, challenges in both the Caribbean and Spain complicated any easy imperialist reliance on the bull.

4.1.2 Montesinos (1511): Hispaniola Dominicans' Prophetic Protest

The first criticism came from Dominican missionaries who arrived in Hispaniola fewer than twenty years after Columbus. They stood collectively against the enslavement of the native peoples, inspiring one conversion whose impact cannot be overstated—as well as heavy argument back in Spain. Dominicans from Salamanca (more on that highly influential university in Part 4.2 below) arrived at the nascent Hispaniola colony in 1510.[179] They were horrified by colonists' enslavement of the Indigenous Taínos (a system known as the *encomienda*).[180]

---

176 Lantigua, *supra* n.42, at 169; *see also* Clement VII, *Indulti Nominandi ad Beneficia & Dignitates Carolo Romanorum & Hispaniarum Regi in Imperatorum Electo*, *reprinted in* Privilegia Nominationum Lovaniensium 76 (Leodij apud Matthiam Hovium 1665) (1529), *available at* https://www.google.com/books/edition/Privilegia_nominationvm_Lovaniensivm/hbsWAAAAQAAJ.

177 *Contrast* G.C. Marks, *Indigenous Peoples in International Law: The Significance of Francisco de Vitoria and Bartolome de las Casas*, 13 Austl. YBIL 1, 40 (1990–91) (arguing that the bull was only spiritual, citing Julius Goebel, The Struggle for the Falkland Islands 84 (2d ed. 1982)).

178 *See* García, *supra* n.147, at 248 ("[A]fter the first 20 years of Spanish presence in the Western Atlantic ... the most important questions concerned the legality, permissibility and morality of what was *de facto* happening in America—namely, a succession of wars and plunders committed against infidels having lived in peace before the arrival of the Spaniards and not being *hostes* [enemies] of the Christians."); Herzog, *supra* n.167, at 25–26 (describing the relationship between *Inter caetera* and possession as "often unclear," with theories "adopted and abandoned according to place, period, and need").

179 *See* Hanke, Struggle, *supra* n.151, at 20; Miguel Anxo Pena González, *The "School of Salamanca" and the American Project*, in Tellkamp, *supra* n.72, at 94 (Carlos Diego Arenas Pacheco trans.) [hereinafter "*American Project*"].

180 *See* Lantigua, *supra* n.42, at 25; Lewis Hanke, Bartolomé de las Casas: An Interpretation of His Life and Writings 15 (1951) ("The Spanish crown gave or 'commended' Indians to Spaniards, who become *encomenderos*, and this grant gave the Spaniards the right to exact labor or tribute .... In return, the *encomenderos* were obliged to provide religious instruction for their Indians and to protect them."), *quoted in* Marks, *supra* n.177, at 21 n.97; David T. Orique, The Unheard Voice of Law in Bartolomé De Las Casas's Brevísima Relación De La Destruición De Las Indias, 94 n.108 (2021) (noting early narration of

"Led by Pedro de Córdoba and their chief preacher Antonio [de] Montesino[s], they prayed and fasted for a year."[181] Then came the last Sunday of Advent, 1511. Montesinos entered a straw-thatched church and preached a jeremiad:

> In order to make your sins against the Indians known to you I have come up on this pulpit, I who am a voice of Christ crying in the wilderness of this island ... this is going to be the strangest voice that you ever heard, the harshest and hardest and most awful and most dangerous that ever you expected to hear. ... This voice says that you are in mortal sin, that you live and die in it, for the cruelty and tyranny you use in dealing with these innocent people. Tell me, by what right or justice do you keep these Indians in such a cruel and horrible servitude? On what authority have you waged a detestable war against these people, who dwelt quietly and peacefully on their own land?[182]

The scandalized colonial governor sent a delegation to the friary to demand Montesinos's expulsion. Córdoba assured them that Montesinos would revisit his theme the next Sunday.[183] He did—but only to escalate the attack. He announced the Dominicans' unanimous decision to excommunicate slaveholders (*encomenderos*), saying "the friars would no more receive them for confession and absolution than if they were so many highway robbers."[184] He told *encomenderos* they could no more be saved than Moors or Turks—Christendom's mortal enemies and the former occupiers of many of the listeners' Spanish homelands.[185] And he welcomed his audience to complain to whomsoever they wanted back in Spain.[186] Virtually nothing more is known about Montesinos's life after this, other than that he returned to Spain to

atrocities by Juan Garcés, an *encomendero* who killed his Indigenous wife, then repented by joining the Dominicans in 1511; he was later killed by Taínos in Venezuela). Regarding the *encomienda's* origins, see Miller, *Chile*, *supra* n.50, at 835–37.

181 Lantigua, *supra* n.42, at 82.

182 *Quoted in* Hanke, Struggle, *supra* n.151, at 17. For part of the sermon in the original Spanish, see *El Sermón de Montesinos*, in Serna, *supra* n.140, at 241–42.

183 *See* Hanke, Struggle, *supra* n.151, at 18.

184 *Quoted in id.*; *see also* Lantigua, *supra* n.42, at 123.

185 *See* Hanke, Struggle, supra n.151, at 19. Serna's version has this appearing in the first homily. *See* Serna, supra n.140, at 242 ("Tened por cierto que en el estado que estáis no os podéis más salvar que los moros o turcos que carecen y no quieren la fe de Jesucristo." ["Be certain that in the state you are in, you can no more be saved than the Moors and Turks who lack and do not want the faith of Jesus Christ."]); *see also id.* at 246–47 (describing second homily).

186 *See* Hanke, Struggle, *supra* n.151, at 18.

advocate for Indigenous rights and was later killed in Venezuela defending them.[187]

We are aware of the shockwaves his homilies caused. Influential historian Lewis Hanke understatedly suggests that Montesinos inspired further inquiry into *Inter caetera*.[188] The deepest personal search we know of was undertaken by a Hispaniola priest who had been an untroubled *encomendero*: the epochal Bartolomé de Las Casas (1474/84–1566).[189] He was not instantly converted; he actually underwent the Dominican excommunication at one point.[190] But two and a half years after Montesinos's entreaties, Las Casas had witnessed a massacre of Taínos in Cuba and, while preparing a homily of his own, read Sirach 34:21–23, which conditions sacrifices on righteousness.[191] He pondered this in his heart for several days, then concluded that "everything done to the Indians thus far was unjust and tyrannical," eventually becoming a Dominican himself.[192] I will discuss Las Casas further below, as he became the most radical Spanish anti-imperialist (see Part 5).

He was not the only one troubled by Montesinos's words. That friar asked "on what authority" the Spaniards warred against the natives. Neither he nor his brothers saw any in *Inter caetera*. The search would soon affect a theologian and a lawyer back in Spain.

4.1.3 Paz (1512–13): Recognizing Indigenous Rights in Canon Law

As Montesinos had anticipated, news of his homilies quickly reached the home country.[193] Ferdinand "held up the departure of the armada" and

---

187 *See id.* at 22.

188 *Id.* at 26.

189 When Las Casas was young, he was present at Columbus's first return to Spain. *See* Clayton & Lantigua, *supra* n.128, at 34. His father sailed on Columbus's third voyage. *See* José Alejandro Cárdenas Bunsen, Escritura y Derecho Canónico en la Obra de Fray Bartolomé de Las Casas 25 (2011).

190 *See* Hanke, Struggle, *supra* n.151, at 21.

191 *See id.*; Rolena Adorno, The Polemics of Possession in Spanish American Narrative 63 (2007).

192 *Quoted in* Hanke, Struggle, *supra* n.151, at 21; *see also* Marks, *supra* n.177, at 21. Las Casas's best-known work chronicles the "devastation" of Indigenous America. For a modern edition, see Bartolomé de Las Casas, An Account, Much Abbreviated, of the Destruction of the Indies with Related Texts (Franklin W. Knight ed., Andrew Hurley trans., Hackett Publ'g Co. 2003) (1552) [hereinafter "Destruction"]. Pagden notes that Las Casas's account of his conversion served a rhetorical purpose, giving his message "a semidivine source" (although I would submit that this is no reason to doubt its authenticity). Anthony Pagden, Ius et Factum*: Text and Experience in the Writings of Bartolomé de Las Casas*, 33 Representations 147, 158 (1991).

193 *See* Serna, *supra* n.140, at 247–51.

convened a *junta*, or formal consultation, at Burgos in 1512–13 to consider the plight of natives and the conquest's legitimacy.[194] Two of the most important participants were Dominican theologian Matías de Paz (*c.*1468/70–1519) and civil lawyer Palacios Rubios.[195] I discuss Paz first. He moved canon law toward recognition of Indigenous rights to peace, property, and labor.

Both Paz and Palacios Rubios relied on medieval authorities, including Innocent, Hostiensis, and the Dominican St. Thomas Aquinas (1224/25–1274).[196] This is not to say that their thinking was retrograde (as some English Protestant writers contended).[197] Rather, Muldoon observes that medieval sources gave Spanish intellectuals "a set of moral standards against which they could measure the activities of the conquistadores before passing judgment on them, as well as a language that could articulate their views."[198]

Neither Paz nor Palacios Rubios was a static receiver of tradition. Reading Aquinas and Innocent in light of new discoveries, they distinguished "islanders

194 Hanke, Struggle, *supra* n.151, at 30; see also Yanay Israeli, *The Requerimiento in the Old World: Making Demands and Keeping Records in the Legal Culture of Late Medieval Castile*, 40 L. & Hist. Rev. 37, 37–38 (2022).

195 *See* García, *supra* n.147, at 238, 249.

196 *See id.*; Birr, *supra* n.174, at 280 ("Reading Palacios Rubios, one can almost overlook the momentousness of the discovery and the otherness of the Americas: The crown jurist adapts the well-established knowledge and legal regimes almost seamlessly to the new situation—on paper, at least. Above all, the Old Testament, Roman and Greek Antiquity as well as the great tradition of medieval jurisprudence seem to offer an extensive toolbox of experiences and knowledge flexible and diverse enough to be applied to the Americas without openly addressing the vast difference in circumstances."). Aquinas started writing his epic Summa Theologiae fifteen years or so after Innocent wrote about infidel *dominium*. *See* Stogre, *supra* n.86, at 52–53.

197 *See* Muldoon, Americas, *supra* n.57, at 169 ("Spain was the wicked, backward, evil empire that flourished only to be destroyed by its own corruption. To English Protestants, Spain deserved to lose her empire because she had sought to impose a reactionary Catholic order on Europe. The treatment of the peoples of the New World illustrated what would happen if the Spanish had remained the dominant power in Europe. The result of this outlook was the Black Legend, which demonized Spanish activities in the New World."); *cf.* Rafael Avira & Alfredo Cruz, *The Controversy between Las Casas and Sepúlveda at Valladolid*, in Hispanic Philosophy in the Age of Discovery at 110 (Kevin White ed., 1997) (observing that Las Casas the medievalist saw Indigenous peoples as far more equal to Europeans than did Juan Ginés de Sepúlveda, a consummate Renaissance humanist). For more on the "Black Legend" of Spanish cruelty and its long shadow over historiography, see William S. Maltby, *Black Legend, The*, in Encyclopedia of Latin American History and Culture, *available at* https://www.encyclopedia.com/humanities/encyclopedias-almanacs-transcripts-and-maps/black-legend.

198 Muldoon, Americas, *supra* n.57, at 170.

'discovered' in the Western Atlantic from the condition of other infidels."[199] Paz saw that Indians "could hardly be said to fit in a framework of concepts and norms constructed to support an unrestricted expansion of Christians over infidels in a context of mutually open hostility."[200] After all, they "happily welcomed the Christian missionaries" and were peaceable.[201] Paz even deemed them ethically innocent of their infidelity because they had never heard of Christianity.[202]

Modern scholar José Luis Egío García goes too far when he says that Paz "cancelled" the logic for colonization.[203] The notion that sinful infidels could be conquered as punishment was only one disputed argument, and *Inter caetera* itself cast Indigenous peoples as happy savages ready to become good Catholics—not criminals.[204] But Paz's understanding attitude did have humanizing consequences. Hanke quotes a key portion of Paz's 1512 work:

> It is not just for Christian Princes to make war on infidels because of a desire to dominate or for their wealth, but only to spread the faith. Therefore, if the inhabitants of those lands never before Christianized wish to listen to and receive the faith, Christian Princes may not invade their territory. ... If an invitation to accept Christianity has not been made, the infidels may justly defend themselves even though the King, moved by Christian zeal and supported by papal authority, has waged just war.

199 García, *supra* n.147, at 249. Paz, like Vitoria after him (whom I discuss below), may have had a personal reason to rethink identity. He was a *converso*—a descendant of converted Spanish Jews—and suffered discrimination in both his academic career and his Dominican religious vocation. *See id.* at 241–44, 249.

200 *Id.* at 247; *see also* McAlister, *supra* n.116, at 454 ("How were the newly found lands to be accommodated to the classical and scriptural knowledge that formed the basis of existing views of the nature of the world? The things that the Europeans found could not be fitted into the fixed and static Aristotelian system of classification.").

201 García, *supra* n.147, at 247.

202 *See id.* at 250. For more regarding the evolution of Spanish thinking about non-Christians, see José Luis Egío, La Consolidación del Estatuto Teológico-Político del Pagano Amerindio en los Maestros 'Salmantinos' y sus Discípulos Novohispanos (1512–1593) (School of Salamanca Working Paper Series 2015-01), *available at* https://publikationen.ub.uni-frankfurt.de/opus4/frontdoor/deliver/index/docId/32404/file/SvSal_WP_2015-01.pdf.

203 García, *supra* n.147, at 250.

204 *See* Muldoon, *Papal Responsibility*, *supra* n.63, at 182 ("It would appear that Alexander basically accepted Innocent IV's views on the right of infidels to *dominium*. At least he did not argue that the mere fact of the natives being infidels would justify conquest."); *Inter caetera*, *supra* n.5, at 76.

> Such infidels may not be held as slaves unless they pertinaciously deny obedience to the prince or refuse to accept Christianity.[205]

Paz did not altogether reject Spanish dominance in the Americas. He wrote about the pope's authority to sanction Castilian rule over Indigenous peoples and, according to an attendee, the Burgos *junta* concluded that Alexander had given the Castilians the authority to seize Indian lands because of native idolatry.[206] Not long after, Spain's 1519 Compilation of the Laws of the Indies straightforwardly declared that the emperor was the perpetual "Lord of the West Indies" because of Alexander's "donation."[207]

Paz supported this conclusion because he found both Hostiensis's *and* Innocent's categorical approaches to infidel *dominium* inadequate—Hostiensis's because "learned men incited Christians to a never-ending war against every kind of infidel and to commit sinful deeds such as massacres and plunders," and Innocent's because it made evangelization and the protection of Christian converts exceptionally difficult.[208] Paz therefore rejected the idea that infidels had political dominion (*dominio regnativo*), as opposed to *dominium* over property and within the family.[209] But he did agree with Innocent's limitation of religious wars to retaking former Christian lands, protecting oppressed believers, and aiding evangelization with indirect coercion.[210] He even excused Indigenous people's "occasional attempts to resist the entry of Christian soldiers and preachers" as resulting from their ignorance that such men "were, in fact, the servants of the True God and the agents of their soon redemption."[211]

Paz also wanted to curb theft, enslavement, and total political subjugation of Indigenous peoples that many "straightforwardly supported."[212] His efforts

---

205 Hanke, Struggle, *supra* n.151, at 27–28 (*quoting* Matías de Paz, Concerning the Rule of the King of Spain over the Indies (1512)).

206 *Id.*; *see also* Lantigua, *supra* n.42, at 68 (citing Martín Fernández de Enciso).

207 *Quoted in* Felipe Castañeda, *Spanish Colonialism as Perpetual Dominion in the Writings of Juan Solórzano Pereira*, in Tellkamp, *supra* n.72).

208 García, *supra* n.147, at 248.

209 *See* Ramón Darío Valdivia Jiménez, *The Pontifical Theocracy of Friar Bartolomé de las Casas, O.P. (1484–1566)* (María José Fernández trans.), in The Transatlantic Las Casas: Historical Trajectories, Indigenous Cultures, Scholastic Thought, and Reception in History at 181 & n.35, 194 (Rady Roldán-Figueroa & David T. Orique eds., 2023).

210 *See* García, *supra* n.147, at 252, 254; *see also id.* at 251 (describing how Paz deemed religious ignorance "an exculpatory force with regards to some of the most elementary precepts that were called upon while waging war against the infidels").

211 *Id.* at 251. Las Casas would extend this logic further, as discussed in Part 5.

212 García, *supra* n.147, at 255; *see also id.* at 249 (discussing Paz's distinctions between *dominium possessorium* and *dominium iurisdictionis*); Mäkinen & Posti, *supra* n.72, at 175 (discussing earlier thinkers' distinctions between the two).

at Burgos contributed to new laws that tried unsuccessfully to reform the *encomiendas*.[213] This effort was not purely altruistic on the Crown's part—it helped check colonial nobility's power.[214] But it was at least partly humanitarian. In addition, Paz's contemporary Dominicans Vicente de Santa María and Reginaldo de Morales promoted his opinions in Mexico;[215] a few natives there became "landowners with European servants" and even occupied "semi-bureaucratic positions" in the colonial administration.[216] Paz qualified whatever mandate for war *Inter caetera* contained and carried forward the tradition of limiting conquest, with some good effect in the colonies.

What about Palacios Rubios? He dealt with Alexander's bull directly and raised it to a central role in Spanish colonization.

4.1.4 Palacios Rubios (1526): the *Requerimiento*'s New Formalism

Paz the theologian approached Burgos with a desire to properly categorize non-Christians. Palacios Rubios the lawyer came wanting to effectively rule them.[217] Following Hostiensis's opinion, Palacios Rubios thought only Alexander could legitimize colonization. He also recognized that war against non-Christians could not be undertaken arbitrarily. So he crafted *Inter caetera* into a legal formula, the *Requerimiento*, which would present Indigenous peoples with a choice: accept divinely granted Spanish authority over them or be subjected by the sword. He meant this as a humanizing measure; it ended up a farce.

Even though *Inter caetera* was issued after Columbus arrived in the West Indies, Palacios Rubios considered it a prerequisite for conquest due to Innocent's reservation to the pope of rights over non-Christians.[218] In fact, he deemed "conquest and occupation" an *obligation* the bull imposed on Castile and a precondition to any rights arising under it.[219] Only the next generation of Spanish

---

213 *See* Hanke, Struggle, *supra* n.151, at 173; Serna, *supra* n.140, at 253–88. The Burgos laws mixed recognition of some Indigenous rights with forced relocations and continued exploitative labor. *See* Miller, *Chile*, *supra* n.50, at 839–40. Indian slavery was not banned until 1573. *See* Hanke, Struggle, *supra* n.151, at 112.

214 Muldoon, Popes, *supra* n.5, at 140.

215 *See* Egío, *supra* n.202, at 28.

216 Pagden, *European Background*, *supra* n.51, at 4; *see also* Pena González, *American Project*, *supra* n.179, at 96 ("[At] the University of Mexico … it was proposed that Indians and the children of Spaniards should study together (although only a handful of Indians would actually study at the University).").

217 Palacios Rubios never visited the West Indies and commanded particular respect precisely because he lacked economic conflicts of interest. *See* Birr, *supra* n.174, at 265. But this lack of perspective left his proposals dangerously idealistic, as discussed below.

218 *See* Lantigua, *supra* n.42, at 62.

219 Birr, *supra* n.174, at 281.

intellectuals, after the Empire had consolidated control, would instead emphasize *Inter caetera*'s evangelization objective.[220]

Palacios Rubios also drew on Hostiensis, believing that because Christ held all power in Heaven and on earth, infidels retained political *dominium* only if they submitted to the pope, who could then depose them.[221] As a corollary, Indigenous peoples had to submit to any "royal power conceded by the papacy in perpetuity"—namely, to the Castilian domination over the Americas granted by *Inter caetera*.[222] To Innocent's requirements that non-Christian rulers admit missionaries and not oppress converts, Palacios Rubios added recognition of Castilian overlordship.[223] He also understood Alexander's bull as granting to Castile the pope's ability to depose native rulers.[224] Many grounds for doing so existed, including a leader's mere non-Christianity.[225] As Birr rues, for Palacios Rubios, reasons for just wars were "never far away."[226]

But the lawyer was not without his humane side: he did criticize *encomiendas*.[227] He also came up with a legal mechanism that, at face value, honored Paz's requirements for the transfer of Indigenous political power: the *Requerimiento*. Yanay Israeli recently wrote about *requerimientos* in other Castilian contexts.[228] They were a "ritual of claim making."[229] They may have drawn some inspiration from pre-jihad warnings used by Muslims (although Israeli doubts this genealogy); in any event, they were part of the canonical tradition of due process.[230] A *requerimiento* required that a claimant appear

220 *See id.*

221 *See* Lantigua, *supra* n.42, at 63–64. Palacios Rubios's opinion was also influenced by his assessment of Indians as too simple to govern themselves. *See id.*

222 *Id.* at 64; *see also Inter caetera*, *supra* n.5, at 74 ("in perpetuum tenore presentium donamus, concedimus, et assignamus, vosque et heredes ac successores"). This technical language signifies a permanent grant.

223 *See* Lantigua, *supra* n.42, at 64, 68.

224 *See* Birr, *supra* n.174, at 275.

225 *See id.* at 277. Birr contends that here, Palacios Rubios interpreted overbroadly canonical authority for freeing Christian slaves from Jewish masters (also a deprivation of *dominium*). *See id.*; *see also* Thomas Aquinas, Summa Theologica II–II, Q. 10, art. 10, resp. (Fathers of Eng. Dominican Prov. trans., 2d ed. 1920), *available at* https://www.newadvent.org/summa/ (allowing for some emancipations: "Nor does the Church harm [Jewish slaveowners] in this, because since those Jews themselves are subject to the Church, she can dispose of their possessions, even as secular princes have enacted many laws to be observed by their subjects, in favor of liberty.").

226 Birr, *supra* n.174, at 272.

227 *Id.*

228 *See generally* Israeli, *supra* n.194.

229 *Id.* at 42.

230 *Id.* at 39, 55–56, 61.

before the addressee with at least two witnesses and a notary, make a demand, and request compliance.[231] The goal was to foreclose ignorance as a defense and give an opportunity for voluntary redress.[232] Castile used *requerimientos* before initiating hostilities.[233]

Palacios Rubios wrote one adapted to American colonization.[234] It declared that God had placed St. Peter at the head of all of humanity, giving him the power to judge and rule all peoples.[235] In turn, one of his papal successors gave Castile the New World.[236] The Indigenous audience had to acknowledge this, as had other natives.[237] If it did not, then the Spanish would war against, enslave, and dispossess it as rebellious—and the listeners would be to blame.[238]

---

231 *See id.* at 42.

232 *See id.* at 46.

233 *See id.* at 45.

234 He apparently received inspiration from "the novice conquistador, lawyer, and geographer Martín Fernández de Enciso" who, speaking to an audience that included Palacios Rubios, "recalled that Moses had sent Joshua 'to require' (*requerir*) the inhabitants of Jericho to abandon their city because God had given to the people of Israel. When they refused, they were decimated." Lantigua, *supra* n.42, at 67–68.

235 *See El Requerimiento, reprinted in* Serna, *supra* n.140, at 299–300 ("... Nuestro Señor dio cargo a uno, que fue llamado San Pedro, para que de todos los hombres del mundo fuese señor y superior, a quien todos obedeciesen y fuese cabeza de todo el linaje humano donde quiera que los hombres viviesen y estuviesen, y en cualquier ley, secta o creencia, y diole a todo el mundo por su reino, señiorío y jurisdicción. ... [M]ás también le permitió que ... juzgar y gobernar a todas las gentes: cristianos, moros, judíos, gentiles y de cualquier otra secta o creencia que fuesen. ... [E]s padre y gobernador de todos los hombres." ["... Our Lord gave charge to one, who was called St. Peter, so that of all the men of the world he would be lord and superior, whom all would obey, and he would be head of the entire human race wherever men would live and be, and of whatever law, sect, or belief, and [the Lord] gave the whole world to [St. Peter's] kingdom, lordship, and jurisdiction .... What is more, he permitted him to ... judge and govern all peoples: Christians, Moors, Jews, Gentiles, and of whatever other sect or belief they were. ... He is the father and governor of all men."]).

236 *See id.* at 300 ("[A]sí que Sus Altezas son Reyes y señores de estas islas y tierra firme, por virtud de la dicha donación ...." ["For this reason, Their Highnesses are Kings and lords of these islands and mainland, by virtue of the said donation"]).

237 *See id.* (saying of other Indigenous people: "han obedecido y servido y sirven como súbditos lo deben hacer ...." ["they have obeyed and served and will serve as subjects have to"]).

238 *See id.* at 301–02 ("Si no lo hicierdes, o en ello dilacion maliciosamente pusierdes, certificos que con el ayuda de Dios yo entraré poderosamente contra vosotros y vos haré guerra por todas las partes y maneras que yo pudiere, y vos sujetaré al yugo y obediencia de la Iglesia y de Sus Altezas, y tomaré vuestras personas y de vuestras mujeres e hijos, y los haré esclavos, y como tales los venderé y dispondré de ellos como Su Alteza mandare, y vos tomaré vuestros bienes y vos haré todos los males y daños que pudiere, como a vasallos que no obedecen ni quieren recibir a su señor y le resisten y contradicen; y protesto que las muertos y daños que de ello se recrecieren sean a vuestra culpa, y no de Su Alteza

This text served several purposes. Theoretically, it afforded Indigenous peoples canonical due process.[239] It shielded the Spanish from any accusation that they followed Hostiensis and denied infidel *dominium* (as they would then need no other justification for war).[240] And—crucially—it revealed that Palacios Rubios and many Spanish imperialists saw *Inter caetera* as conferring legal authority at least as much as religious jurisdiction, because it required submission to Castilian rule more than conversion to Catholicism.[241]

Starting in 1526, the *Requerimiento* had to be read, by interpreters, as many times as was necessary for it to be understood. And *conquistadores* had to partner with clerics, who had to consent to any war in writing and could revoke licenses to conquer. These were not entirely empty threats. At least one sixteenth-century *conquistador*, Juan Pérez de Cabrera, abandoned a conquest because Guatemalan authorities followed these regulations strictly.[242]

But the *Requerimiento* was usually employed frivolously—to the point of absurdity. Las Casas "could not decide whether to laugh or cry" after witnessing it being read.[243] It was almost always read in Castilian or Latin, without the required translation.[244] Gonzalo Fernández de Oviedo (1478–1557), acting as a notary, saw it proclaimed to natives who were enchained.[245] Neither the reader nor the listeners understood the text, and when someone did finally translate it, the Spanish did not wait for a reply, but instead beat with a stick those who

ni mía ...." ["If you do not do this, or maliciously delay, I assure you that with the help of God I will forcefully enter against you and war against you in all places and manners I can, and I will subject you to the yoke and obedience of the Church and Their Highnesses, and take your people and your women and sons, and make them slaves, and as such I will sell them and dispose of them as His Highness mandates, and I will take from you also your goods and I will inflict on you all the evils and injuries I will be able to, as to vassals who do not obey nor want to receive their lord and resist and contradict him; and I protest that the deaths and injuries that result from this will be your fault, and not His Highness's or mine"]).

239 *See* Israeli, *supra* n.194, at 47, 61–62.

240 *See* Muldoon, Americas, *supra* n.57, at 27; Muldoon, *Requerimiento*, *supra* n.77, at 313 (contending that the document was an "effort to prove to the papacy that ... the primary reason for the conquest ... was to convert and to civilize the natives. It was not undertaken for base motives."); Muldoon, Popes, *supra* n.5, at 141 ("The point of the *Requerimiento* ... was that the infidels did have *dominium* and that the Spanish had to justify their invasion by demonstrating the unwillingness of the Indians to admit peaceful missionaries.").

241 Muldoon, Popes, *supra* n.5, at 138.

242 *See* Hanke, Struggle, *supra* n.151, at 111–12.

243 McAlister, *supra* n.116, at 90.

244 *See id.*

245 Hanke, Struggle, *supra* n.151, at 34.

moved along too slowly.[246] Oviedo sarcastically proposed caging Indians so they would have enough time to comprehend it.[247]

What he saw was something of a marquee performance. At other times, Indians could not be located, so the *Requerimiento* was "read to trees and empty huts."[248] Hanke recounts other instances of palpable bad faith:

> Captains muttered its theological phrases into their beards on the edge of sleeping Indian settlements, or even a league away before starting the formal attack, and at times some leather-lunged Spanish notary hurled its sonorous phrases after the Indians as they fled into the mountains. Once it was read in camp before the soldiers to the beat of the drum. Ship captains would sometimes have the document read from the deck as they approached an island, and at night would send out enslaving expeditions, whose leaders would shout the traditional Castilian war cry "Santiago!" rather than read the Requirement before they attacked the near-by villages. Sometimes Indian messengers were sent to "require" other Indians.[249]

Accounts of instances where Indigenous listeners *did* understand show that they were unpersuaded. One *conquistador* recalled a group of natives responding that monotheism "seemed well and good, and this is how things must be," but: (1) if Alexander had given them over to the Castilians, he "must have been drunk," because "he was 'bestowing' something that was not his"; (2) Ferdinand had to have been unhinged in even asking for the grant, "since he was requesting something that belonged to someone else"; and (3) the Indians would not yield because "they were lords of their land and ... there was no need of another."[250]

---

246 *See id.*

247 *See* McAlister, *supra* n.116, at 90.

248 Hanke, Struggle, *supra* n.151, at 34.

249 *Id.*

250 *Quoted in* Gutiérrez, *supra* n.125, at 122; *see also* Muldoon, Americas, *supra* n.57, 113 ("[T]he Italian traveler [Rutilio Benzoni] told of the king of the Peruvians, one Atabalibam, who, when informed by a Spaniard that the pope had awarded his kingdom to the King of Spain, responded: 'The pope is remarkably foolish and impudent to have handed [it] over to him so easily because he bestows freely [that which belongs] to another.'").

Mantilla rightly deems it "a tragedy that there are no records of Aymara, Quechua, Maya, Aztec, and other Indigenous thinkers' views on the application of normative standards to the international relations between diverse civilizations." Mantilla, *Tawantinsuyu*, *supra* n.162, at 297. Some manuscript destruction took place before the arrival of Europeans. *See* María Castañeda de La Paz, *Itzcóatl y Los Instrumentos de Su Poder*, 36 Estudios de Cultura

Due in part to abusive use of the *Requerimiento*, Palacios Rubios is often villainized. This is somewhat anachronistic. Las Casas called Palacios Rubios a good man, good Christian, and benevolent to Indians, and credited the lawyer for helping him.[251] In the end, though, whatever his personal merits, Palacios Rubios put *Inter caetera* at the heart of a project of brutal conquest. His *Requerimiento* was recited in the field for decades.[252] The papal history and threats of dire punishments were removed in 1543, but it took another thirty years for Spain to formally rebrand its campaign one of "pacification" and not "conquest."[253] Whatever may have been happening in high Spanish discourse, Alexander's *Inter caetera* became Palacios Rubios's dark incantation, spoken intelligibly or muttered in a strange tongue, that heralded empire and its bloodshed wherever they went.

4.1.5 Evaluating *Inter caetera* in the Early Era: Sanction, Scorn, and Sanction Again

Understandings of Alexander's bull evolved dramatically during the early stages of colonial conquest. Despite the contextual complexities in its background, Spaniards **initially** understood *Inter caetera* as obvious backing for their imperial endeavors. **Montesinos** and the Hispaniola Dominicans exploded in protest at the ensuing devastation of Indigenous peoples. Back in Spain, **Paz** responded by discerning limits to conquest (like those found in the earlier canonical tradition as well). But the harsher interpretation of *Inter caetera* returned with a vengeance: **Palacios Rubios** may have meant well, but his *Requerimiento* turned its concepts into the blade of the *conquistador*'s sword.

More evils followed, calling *Inter caetera*'s very legitimacy into question.

Náhuatl 115, 120 (2005). The *conquistadores* then destroyed books systematically. *See* Lori Boornazian Diel, *Nahua and Mixtec Pictorial Books: Religion and History through Visual Text*, in The Oxford Handbook of Mesoamerican Archaeology 869 (Deborah L. Nichols & Christopher A. Pool eds., 2012); Adorno, *supra* n.191, at 212 ("[T]he native Mexican codices had been systematically destroyed by the first archbishop of Mexico, Fray Juan de Zumárraga, and, according to period sources, the native Mexican lords took it upon themselves to voluntarily destroy codices they owned, out of fear of being charged with idolatry for possessing them."). Spanish Franciscan friar Bernardino de Sahagún (1499–1590) did overcome significant colonial opposition and undertake ethno-linguistic research in Mexico, frequently letting "the Amerindian voices speak for themselves." Adorno, *supra* n.191, at 209; *see also* H. B. Nicholson, *Fray Bernardino de Sahagún: A Spanish Missionary in New Spain, 1529–1590*, in Representing Aztec Ritual: Performance, Text, and Image in the Work of Sahagún (Eloise Quiñones Keber ed., 2002). But the historical record is still missing many of the voices of the *Requerimiento's* recipients.

251 Birr, *supra* n.174, at 265 ("*favorecedor de los indios*").

252 *See* Muldoon, *Requerimiento*, *supra* n.77, at 314.

253 Hanke, Struggle, *supra* n.151, at 112, 131.

4.2 *An Unfinished Revolution (1539): Vitoria's Turn to Natural Law*

Palacios Rubios's marriage of *Inter caetera* to brutality proved too much for many Spaniards. Learning of fresh atrocities, Vitoria would deny that Alexander had the authority to grant Spain its colonies. He would not reject imperialism outright, but instead rethink it from first principles of natural law, proposing new limits on conquest.

Conquistadores soon moved from the beachheads into the interior. They found societies far more complex and powerful than those of the Taínos and Caribs, but did not alter their cruel method of approach. In 1532, *conquistador* Francisco Pizarro, holding Spanish grants,[254] attacked the Incan city of Cajamarca.[255] He used preemptive strikes, massacred civilians, and tortured captives.[256] His comrade Vicente de Valverde then presented the Incan emperor Atahuallpa (*c.*1502–1533) with the *Requerimiento*, which Atahuallpa rejected by throwing away Valverde's Bible.[257] The *conquistadores* attacked again, slaughtering Incan officials and civilians.[258] They kidnapped Atahuallpa, then executed him *after* he paid his supposed ransom.[259] Legal niceties meant little to the men scaling the Andes in search of gold.[260]

Many Spaniards were aghast.[261] Vitoria (*c.*1486–1546) wrote a letter to a fellow Dominican voicing his outrage:

---

254 *See* Yuri G. Mantilla, *Francisco de Vitoria's Normative Ideas and the Beginnings of International Law: A Colonial Ethnocentric Discourse, or a Bona Fide Effort to Construct Just International Norms?*, 44 Loy. L.A. Int'l & Comp. L. Rev. 339, 351 (2021) [hereinafter "Vitoria"].

255 Mantilla, *Tawantinsuyu*, *supra* n.162, at 309.

256 *See id.* at 309–10.

257 *See id.* at 316–17, 321.

258 *See id.* at 317, 321.

259 *See id.* at 322.

260 *See id.* at 317, 320, 323.

261 Inspired directly by Cajamarca or not, five years later, Pope Paul III (r. 1534–1549) issued a bull, *Sublimis Deus*, declaring that Indigenous peoples "are by no means to be deprived of their liberty or the possession of their property, even though they be outside the faith of Jesus Christ," and "should the contrary happen, it shall be null and have no effect." Paul III, *Sublimis Deus* (May 29, 1537), *reprinted in Appendix B to* Panzer, *supra* n.95, at 81; *see also id.* (the key Latin being: "sua libertate ac rerum suarum dominio privatos seu privandos non esse .... nec in servitutem redigi debere"). For more regarding Paul's role in defending Indigenous rights and attempting to abolish Indian slavery, see Panzer, *supra* n.95, at 16–28; Stogre, *supra* n.86, at 80–93, 115–16 & n.38. *Sublimis Deus* was one of many papal documents cited by the Holy See's UN Permanent Observer Mission as invalidating *Inter caetera*. *See* Boyd, *supra* n.34; Perm. Obs. Miss. of the Holy See, *supra* n.31, at 1. Many of these are reprinted in English and Latin in *Appendix B to* Panzer, *supra* n.95. But as Egío and Birr note regarding Eugene's intervention on behalf of the Guanche, these measures defended *dominium rerum*—freedom of labor and property—not necessarily *dominium iurisdictionis*, or political authority. *See* Egío & Birr, *Before Vitoria*, *supra* n.114,

> I understand from eyewitnesses who were personally present during the recent battle with Atahuallpa, neither he nor any of his people had ever done the slightest injury to the Christians, nor given them the least grounds for making war on them. ... But even supposing the justice in the war is all on the side of the Spaniards, hostilities may not proceed beyond subduing them and compelling them to accept the emperor as prince with the infliction on them of as little damage and loss as possible. This does not mean robbing them and leaving them destitute of everything regarding their temporal goods. ... In truth, if the Indians are not men but monkeys, they are incapable of injury. But if they are men, and our neighbors, and as they claim vassals of the emperor, I cannot see how to excuse these conquistadors of utter impiety and tyranny; nor can I see what great service they do to His Majesty by ruining his vassals.[262]

Vitoria's letter reveals his desire to unite criticism of colonial evils with acceptance of empire. His developments of natural-law thought would serve the first purpose. For his contemporaries and successors, a reimagined role for *Inter caetera* would serve the second.

Vitoria was a Dominican and the prime chair in theology at the University of Salamanca in western Spain from 1526 (the year the *Requerimiento* was made obligatory) until his death in 1546.[263] During this time, Salamanca became the center of Spanish intellectual life. Vitoria and his colleagues crafted an intellectual renaissance based on the thought of Aquinas.[264] His interlocutors and students developed a worldwide network that changed how the Spanish

---

at 56–57; Stogre, *supra* n.86, at 97–104. Additionally, Charles revoked *Sublimis Deus* within his realms because it did not follow imperial approval procedures. *See* Hanke, *supra* n.151, at 150.

262 Letter of Francisco de Vitoria to Miguel Arcos, OP (Nov. 8, 1534), in Francisco de Vitoria: Political Writings 331–33 (Anthony Pagden & Jeremy Lawrance eds., 1991), *quoted in* Mantilla, *Tawantinsuyu*, *supra* n.162, at 315–16.

263 *See* Bernice Margaret Hamilton, *Francisco de Vitoria*, Britannica, https://www.britannica.com/biography/Francisco-de-Vitoria; Hanke, Struggle, *supra* n.151, at 111.

264 *See* Pena González, *American Project*, *supra* n.179, at 84–85, 89; *see also* Daniel Allemann, Spreading the Faith to American Indians: Alfonso de Castro's Call for Amerindian Education in the Context of the Second Scholastic at 9 (School of Salamanca Working Paper Series 2015-05), available at https://publikationen.ub.uni-frankfurt.de/opus4/frontdoor/deliver/index/docId/37612/file/SvSal_WP_2015-05.pdf ("The neo-scholastic theologians not only based their treatment of natural law on Aquinas but enlarged his juridical vocabulary by also drawing on 'later medieval conceptions of rights as belonging to the individual' and thereby they generated a juridical framework with which they could address 'the competing claims of states, subjects, and non-subjects in a rapidly-changing world.'" (citation omitted)).

understood their world mission. The School of Salamanca has even been credited with founding "the modern law of nations."[265] Thomas Duve explains their interconnections:

> [P]riests and missionaries, theologians and jurists, royal officials and merchants were part of a communicative community that was not restricted to certain cities, regions, or continents, but whose books, letters, reports, and similar things circulated in an enormous space. These all contributed to the translation, in similar contexts and sometimes quite distinct ones, of a juridical-political language that took Salamanca as one of their principal centers of production, albeit not in an exclusive way.[266]

Salamancans united Spain, Mexico City, Lima, and Manila, fostering intellectual "co-evolution" toward a "'universal code' of legality" applicable throughout the Empire.[267]

Vitoria's recovery of Thomism led to new political ideas. For Aquinas, political authority comes directly from human nature, not by way of religious authority.[268] He considers politics a form of social cooperation arising from universal human reason. Humans live in societies "so that each one may assist his fellows."[269] Every society has to make reasoned decisions about what "is best for itself"; a key one is who will govern.[270] Aquinas says that moderate, responsible, conscientious people—Christian or not—should be able "to choose

265 9 J. B. Scott, The Spanish Origin of International Law (1932), *quoted in* Marks, *supra* n.177, at 8.

266 Thomas Duve, La Escuela de Salamanca: ¿Un Caso de Producción Global de Conocimiento?: Consideraciones Introductorias desde una Perspectiva Histórico-Jurídica y de la Historia del Conocimiento, at 19 (School of Salamanca Working Paper Series 2018-02), *available at* https://publikationen.ub.uni-frankfurt.de/opus4/frontdoor/deliver/index/docId/37615/file/SvSal_WP-2018-02.pdf (original in Spanish); *see also* Cervera, *supra* n.167, at 4 ("Many of the missionaries trained or influenced by the School of Salamanca ... all had a common vision of the world. That vision of the world, at the same time, was transformed.").

267 Duve, *supra* n.266, at 14, 28 (original in Spanish).

268 *See* Xavier Foccroulle Ménard & Anna Su, *Liberalism, Integralism, and the Question of Religious Freedom*, 47 BYU L. Rev. 1171, 1185 (2022). I discuss Aquinas's political thought more in an article in *Politics and Religion, Early Stirrings of Modern Liberty in the Thought of St. Thomas Aquinas*, available at https://www.cambridge.org/core/journals/politics-and-religion/article/early-stirrings-of-modern-liberty-in-the-thought-of-st-thomas-aquinas/767553BEC40952984E8DB03F49EA1DBC. Parts of my discussion here follow it.

269 Thomas Aquinas, De Regno ad Regem Cypri paras. 5–6 (Gerald B. Phelan & I. Th. Eschmann trans., 1949), *available at* https://isidore.co/aquinas/DeRegno.htm [hereinafter "De Regno"].

270 Aquinas, Summa Theologica I–II, *supra* n.226, Q. 95, art. 4, resp..

their own magistrates."[271] Thomism's naturalism and universalism are why Pagden wrote that "all extended empires" existed in tension with Salamancans' sense of "the true nature of the civil community."[272] Thomists certainly agreed with Innocent that infidels can have *dominium*.[273]

Building from his Thomist worldview and conviction that evil had happened in Peru, Vitoria complicated Spanish colonialism. He tries to balance the fact that the Empire was run by "men who are alike well-informed and upright" against the reality of "so many massacres, so many plunderings, so many princes evicted from their possessions and stripped of their rule."[274] He begins by considering Innocent and Hostiensis on infidel *dominium*.[275] He agrees with Innocent, adding Thomist reasons: not believing in Christianity "does not destroy either natural law or human law; but ownership and dominion are based either on natural or on human law; therefore they are not destroyed by want of faith."[276] Because *dominium* is a natural right, neither "unbelief or any other mortal sin" lets Christians seize it.[277] The fact that natives may have sim-

271 *Id.* Q. 97, art. 1, resp.; *see also* Aquinas, De Regno, *supra* n.269, para. 31 (discussing pagan Rome).

272 Pagden, Lords, *supra* n.44, at 49. Pagden says that the Salamancans were primarily concerned with European disputes. *See id.* But Vitoria and others wrote lengthily on Indian affairs, and Salamanca alumni worked in the American and Philippine colonies; overseas issues were no sideshow for them. *See* Mantilla, *Vitoria, supra* n.254, at 359 ("[Vitoria's] rejection of the pope and European emperor's authority in the New World is of central importance."); Lantigua, *supra* n.42, at 10 ("The juridical locus of international society for ... the Spanish Dominicans was ... the European encounter with infidels in a New World.").

273 Not least because, by Vitoria's day, Martin Luther (1483–1546) had taught that *dominium* is conferred by divine grace, not through natural law. *See* Pagden, *Dispossessing, supra* n.72, at 87. For late-medieval thought about *dominium, see* Dickason, *supra* n.72, at 165–69.

274 Francisco de Vitoria, De Indis et de Iure Belli Relectiones, *reprinted in* The Classics of International Law 119 (James Brown Scott ed., John Pawley Bate trans., Carnegie Inst. of Wash. 1917) [hereinafter "De Indis"]. This edition contains a photographic reprint of a 1696 printing of the original Latin beginning at page 299. These *relectiones* originated as lectures Vitoria delivered at Salamanca in 1539. *See* Barbara Diaz Kayel, *Los 'Justos Títulos' de España al Dominio de América: La* Relectio de Indis *de Francisco de Vitoria y Su Influencia en la Legislación Indiana*, 5 Revista de la Facultad de Derecho (Uru.) 67, 82 (2005).

275 *See* Vitoria, De Indis, *supra* n.274, at 120. Lantigua also names the influential Dominican Tommaso de Vio ("Cardinal Cajetan") (1468/69–1534) as inspiring Vitoria here. *See* Lantigua, *supra* n.42, at 77–78, 86–92, 96–99, 103, 110, 113, 130; *Cajetan*, Britannica, https://www.britannica.com/biography/Cajetan.

276 Vitoria, De Indis, *supra* n.274, at 123.

277 *See id.* at 125; *see also* Allemann, *supra* n.264, at 17 ("[E]xactly because the Spanish Thomists conceived *dominium* as natural right that was exclusively grounded in the reasoning of natural law, they refused the view that sin or unbelief could have any effect on

pler societies than Europeans does not eliminate their human rights; besides, they have well-organized societies, laws, and economies (by now, Spain had encountered the Aztecs, Inca, and Maya).[278] Vitoria also echoes Paz's Thomist framework of "innocent infidelity," contending that "it is through no fault of theirs that these aborigines have for many centuries been outside the pale of salvation."[279] That makes it even less appropriate to dispossess them than it would be to deny natural rights to Muslims and Jews, who enjoy them within European Christendom.[280]

Vitoria also dismisses several other grounds for colonization. First, in spite of the emperor's ties to ancient Rome,[281] he is not "lord of the whole earth"; even if he were, as Paz says, he would hold *dominium* only in jurisdiction, not

a human being's true *dominium*. Consequently, they rejected the idea that the papal bulls granted to the Catholic Monarchs could be used as a justification of Spanish *dominium* in the New World.").

278 *See* Vitoria, De Indis, *supra* n.274, at 127–28. "In broadly unique colonial patterns, whereas the Spanish sought to incorporate '*indios*' within the political rule of transatlantic Christendom, the English mostly displaced nonpropertied 'savages' to make room for Western civilization." Lantigua, *supra* n.42, at 52. This tracks a broader difference in emphasis between English dominion over land and Spanish rule over people. "When Locke and other English colonists gazed at native inhabitants to determine if they had property in the earth itself and money, they concluded that its absence meant natives did not have organized political authority. In contrast, the Spanish Dominican theologians, using a variation of Aristotle's political taxonomy, observed the rational characteristics of Amerindian city life with rulers, marriages, laws, commerce, and religion." *Id.* at 268.

Scholar Yuri Mantilla recently defended Vitoria from charges of ethnocentrism. *See* generally Mantilla, *Vitoria, supra* n.254. Shawnee/Lenape scholar Steven T. Newcomb accuses Vitoria based on a passage describing Indians as unintelligent, primitive, uncivilized, and childlike. *See* Newcomb, *Evidence, supra* n.19, at 313. But Vitoria clarifies that he, who had never been to the Americas, thinks this opinion could "not be asserted, but [only] brought up for discussion," and "dare[s] not affirm" nor "entirely condemn" it. Vitoria, De Indis, *supra* n.274, at 160–61; *see also* Mantilla, *Vitoria, supra* n.254, at 367; Bartolomé de Las Casas, In Defense of the Indians: The Defense of the Most Reverend Lord, Don Fray Bartolomé de Las Casas, of the Order of Preachers, Late Bishop of Chiapa, Against the Persecutors and Slanderers of the Peoples of the New World Discovered Across the Seas 341 (Stafford Poole trans., N. Ill. Univ. Press 1992) [hereinafter Defense] ("[Vitoria] is a little more careless … since he wished to moderate what seemed to the Emperor's party to have been rather harshly put …. He indicates this well enough by speaking conditionally, fearing that he might suppose or make false statements instead of true ones."). Despite Vitoria's caveats, some have traced the twentieth-century League of Nations' paternalistic "mandate" system to this passage. *See* Marks, *supra* n.177, at 47 (mentioning J. B. Scott in this regard).

279 Vitoria, De Indis, *supra* n.274, at 127.

280 *See id.* at 128.

281 See Pagden, Lords, *supra* n.44, at 26–27, and McAlister, *supra* n.116, at 293 for discussion of the Spanish reception of the Roman idea of universal sovereignty.

ownership, so he would err in "converting provinces to his own use or in giving towns or even estates away at his pleasure."[282] Second, the pope "is not civil or temporal lord of the whole world."[283] Vitoria rejects the Donation of Constantine and the *Requerimiento*.[284] He notes that some people see the pope as having "free power" to "make the Kings of Spain rulers over the Indian aborigines"; alternatively, they say that "if these aborigines refused to recognize the temporal power of the Pope over them, this would warrant him in making war on them and in putting rulers over them."[285] But even in spiritual matters, where papal power is at its zenith, the pope lacks jurisdiction over non-Christians. He cannot excommunicate them, nor regulate their marriages to the same degree as he can those of the faithful. Even less so does he have temporal power over infidels' politics, even to curb serious sins like cannibalism, incest, or sodomy.[286] And even if he had such power, he could not confer it on secular rulers, as it would "be annexed to the Papacy."[287] Therefore, Indigenous people's refusal to yield before the *Requerimiento* "furnishes no ground for making war on them and seizing their property."[288]

This is especially so because neither the truth of Christianity nor derivative beliefs about papal authority can be proven readily through natural reason.[289] Worse, the presence of "many scandals and cruel crimes and acts of impiety"

---

282 Vitoria, De Indis, *supra* n.274, at 131–33; *see also* García, *supra* n.147, at 249.

283 Vitoria, De Indis, *supra* n.274, at 135; *see also id.* at 240 (the Latin). For the earlier, contrary opinion of canonist Joannes Andreae (*c.*1270–1348), see Brian Tierney, Foundations of the Conciliar Theory: The Contribution of the Medieval Canonists from Gratian to the Great Schism 199–200 (1955).

284 *See* Lantigua, *supra* n.42, at 98; Mantilla, *Tawantinsuyu*, *supra* n.162, at 319 (noting that Vitoria's rebuttal stylistically tracks the *Requerimiento*).

285 Vitoria, De Indis, *supra* n.274, at 135; *see also id.* at 240 (the Latin).

286 *See id.* at 136, 145–46; *see also id.* at 253 ("Item mirum est quod Papa non possit ferre leges infidelibus et possit exercere iudicia et inferre poenas." ["Also notable is that the Pope cannot enact laws over infidels, but can exercise judgment and impose penalties."]); Mantilla, Vitoria, supra n.254, at 388 ("For Vitoria … [o]nly the gravest violations of natural law, such as the killing of innocent persons, justified the use of force."); Andreas Wagner, *Francisco de Vitoria*, in Great Christian Jurists in Spanish History 94 (Rafael Domingo & Javier Martínez-Torrón eds., 2018) ("The political self-determination of a people, and hence the possibilities of radical otherness having no effect on legal standing in the international realm, extended even to spiritual matters: For Vitoria … [idolatry being evil] did not mean that some foreign agent could possess the authority to intervene and remedy the situation."). Jurist Gregorio López (1496–1560) was an early critic on this point, defending Innocent's assertion of papal authority to punish crimes against natural law. *See* Barrientos, *supra* n.5, at 63–64.

287 Vitoria, De Indis, supra n.273, at 136; see also id. at 241 (the Latin).

288 *Id.* at 137; *see also id.* at 243 (the Latin).

289 *See id.* at 138, 140–45.

by the Spanish, together with "no miracles or signs or religious patterns of life," makes it only natural that Indians will not convert.[290] Besides, even disbelief in the face of *adequate* proof of Christianity does not justify war,[291] because fear makes any conversions that result involuntary and so sacrilegious.[292] (Note that Vitoria was Paz's fellow *converso*, a descendant of converted Spanish Jews. He lived after the *Reconquista* and its expulsion of unconverted Jews and Muslims.[293])

Vitoria concludes, then, that the *Requerimiento* does not legitimize colonization. The manner in which it is delivered certainly does not help: "[F]ear and ignorance, which vitiate every choice, ought to be absent. But they were markedly operative … for the Indians did not know what they were doing; nay, they may not have understood what the Spaniards were seeking."[294] But not even perfect recitation can cure the more fundamental problems for Vitoria the Thomist: Indigenous peoples cannot replace their sovereigns without good reason, and Indigenous sovereigns cannot accept new overlords without popular consent.[295]

Noteworthily in light of the modern conflation of different rationales for colonialism, Vitoria also dismisses any "right of discovery," noting that America was already inhabited when the Spanish arrived.[296] He summarily concludes that discovery "gives no support to a seizure of the aborigines any more than

290 *Id.* at 144. Las Casas will echo this argument, as I discuss in Part 5 below.

291 Vitoria has a restrained view of just war. *See id.* at 170 (rejecting religious difference and imperial ambition as justifications), 173 (requiring "that an exceedingly careful examination be made of the justice and causes of the war and that the reasons of those who on grounds of equity oppose it be listened to."); Francisco de Vitoria, Relectio de Potestate Civili: Estudios Sobre Su Filosofía Política 44 (Jesús Cordero Pando ed., Consejo Superior de Investigaciones Científicas 2008) (1528) [hereinafter "De Potestate Civili"] ("[N]am respublica non habet potestatem bellum inferendi nisi ad se resque suas tuendas atque protegendum." ["No republic has the power to make war except to protect itself and its affairs."]).

292 *See* Vitoria, De Indis, *supra* n.274, at 144; *see also id.* at 250–51 ("Timor autem multum minuit de voluntario et ex timore servili dumtaxat accedere ad mysteria et sacramenta Christi sacrilegum est." (internal citation omitted) ["Great fear lessens voluntariness and it is a sacrilege to come to the mystery and sacrament of Christ entirely out of servile fear"]).

293 *See* García, *supra* n.147, at 241–44, 249.

294 Vitoria, De Indis, *supra* n.274, at 148; *see also id.* at 254 (the Latin).

295 *See id.*; *see also* Vitoria, De Potestate Civili, *supra* n.291, at 24–25, 200–01 (containing Vitoria's analysis of a society's right to govern itself and his commentary on Aquinas concluding that a sovereign cannot serve the good of a foreign republic to the detriment of his own); Lantigua, *supra* n.42, at 99 (discussing these points).

296 Vitoria, De Indis, *supra* n.274, at 138; *see also id.* at 244 (the Latin).

if it had been they who had discovered us."[297] He holds that "at the time of the Spaniards' first voyages to America they took with them no right to occupy the lands of the Indigenous population."[298]

Despite all this, Vitoria does not conclude that the Empire must withdraw back to Europe. Instead, he maintains that the law of nations (*ius gentium*) grants all people the right to travel and trade freely anywhere in the world, as long as they do no harm.[299] (He does not mention theft the Spaniards had committed in the New World, despite their seizing many precious minerals, because of what he takes to be international norms regarding unappropriated resources.[300]) Denial of travel and trade rights should be met first with "reason and persuasion," especially because Indigenous peoples may naturally

297 *Id.* at 139.

298 *Id.* at 138; *see also id.* at 244 (the Latin).

299 *See id.* at 151–52; *see also id.* at 162 (noting, though, that the Portuguese traded with Indigenous peoples "without reducing them to subjection"); *id.* at 268 (the Latin). For Vitoria's explanation of why *ius gentium* is universally binding, even on Indigenous peoples, *see* Vitoria, De Potestate Civili, *supra* n.291, at 62–65. Likely considering Spain's hopes for universal monarchy, Vitoria does think that the law of nations allows a majority of Christians to elect a single sovereign over all *Christendom. See* Pagden, Lords, *supra* n.44, at 41. But before that sovereign could reign over all humanity, a majority of it would have to consent. *See id.* at 47.

Later Protestant jurist Samuel Pufendorf (1632–1694) reasonably criticized Vitoria's right to travel as requiring open borders: "[I]t is crude indeed to try to give others so indefinite a right to journey and live among us, with no thought of the numbers in which they come, their purpose in coming, as well as of the question whether, in passing through without harm and visiting a foreign land, they propose to stay but a short time, or to settle among us permanently ...." 8 Samuel Pufendorf, De Jure Naturae et Gentium 364–65 (C. H. Oldfather & William Abbott trans., 1934) (1672), *quoted in* Mantilla, *Vitoria, supra* n.254, at 363; *see also id.* at 376 ("Vitoria did not consider that even the peaceful presence of Spanish people in indigenous territories could have been hurtful to the preservation of indigenous nations and their cultures."); Pagden, *Dispossessing, supra* n.72, at 89–90 (noting rejection of Vitoria's sweeping right to travel by his own student, Melchor Cano (*c.*1509–1560)); Marks, *supra* n.177, at 44 (contrasting that Las Casas knew "of the potentially devastating effect on the Indians of co-existence with the Spaniards (whose activities were rarely restricted to simple trade), and he opposed the imposition of obligations on the Indians to allow free intercourse.").

To Vitoria's credit, he did condition travel and trade rights on factual circumstances and a lack of harm. *See* Vitoria, De Indis, *supra* n.274, at 158; *id.* at 264 (the Latin); Mantilla, *Vitoria, supra* n.254, at 374–75 ("[F]or Vitoria, the normative principle of natural partnership and communication, which was the foundation for the norms of travel and trade, did not apply when the Spaniards injured indigenous people. ... Because of this, Vitoria used the scholastic dialectic method to balance the application of the norms of the natural law of nations with exceptions for their implementation.").

300 *See* Vitoria, De Indis, *supra* n.274, at 153. Mantilla rightly criticizes Vitoria as naïve here, too. *See* Mantilla, *Vitoria, supra* n.254, at 364–65.

fear armed, powerful strangers. But if that does not avail, the Spanish can wage "purely defensive" war—"so far as possible with the least damage to the natives."[301] Vitoria also accepts the Spanish seizing control of Indigenous societies if this is strictly necessary to ensure colonists' safety.[302]

He also identifies a related right of Christians to preach the Gospel everywhere, and of everyone to practice the faith freely if they so choose—rights whose violation can justify proportionate war as a last resort.[303] In such cases, the Spanish exercise a natural right of protecting the oppressed which, notably, does not depend on papal authorization.[304] Additionally, if many Indians become Christians, the pope can appoint a believing sovereign and depose infidel ones, in line with canon law.[305]

As a separate matter, Vitoria approves of wars to stop Indigenous tyranny and human sacrifice, including by occupying societies long enough to fully eradicate that practice.[306] This proved potent support for imperialism. Vitoria

---

301 Vitoria, De Indis, *supra* n.274, at 154–55; *see also id.* at 260–61 (the Latin).

302 *See id.* at 155; *id.* at 261 (the Latin); *id.* at 171 ("[A] prince may ... do whatever is necessary in order to obtain peace and security from the enemy ....").

303 *See id.* at 156–57; *see also id.* at 158; *id.* at 264 (the Latin).

304 *See id.* at 156–57; *id.* at 263 (the Latin); *see also* Mantilla, Vitoria, *supra* n.254, at 385 ("On one hand, it seems that he used ethical and legal norms to justify Spain's imperial expansion. On the other hand, it seems that he applied what he considered to be just and universal norms to help indigenous people who suffered oppression and persecution ...."). Marks has noted similar controversies in our own time. *See* Marks, *supra* n.177, at 45 n.201 ("Very similar issues arise in the modem discussion of recognition of customary law in the context of indigenous rights eg discussion of traditionally sanctioned killing, or punishment which may appear inhumane and cruel, and thus in opposition to universal standards contained in instruments such as the [International Covenant on Civil and Political Rights]."). Queen Isabella relied partly on humanitarian intervention in enslaving cannibal Caribs. *See* Lantigua, *supra* n.42, at 61.

305 *See* Vitoria, De Indis, *supra* n.274, at 159; *see also id.* at 162 (contending that the spread of Christianity among Indigenous peoples had made Spanish withdrawal from the Americas unwise); Muldoon, *Colonial Charters*, *supra* n.50, at 377; Muldoon, Americas, *supra* n.57, at 132–33; Egío, *supra* n.202, at 57–58 (noting "theological (even if not theocratic)" justification for imperialism, which would be "exercised in a totally disinterested form: that is to say, giving absolute priority" to evangelization (translation mine)). However, Vitoria did not think the pope could appoint a replacement for a deposed ruler: the power of election belonged to the people by natural law. *See* Lewis Hanke, All Mankind is One: A Study of the Disputation Between Bartolomé de Las Casas and Juan Ginés de Sepúlveda in 1550 on the Intellectual and Religious Capacity of the American Indians 103 (1974) [hereinafter "Mankind"].

306 *See* Vitoria, De Indis, *supra* n.274, at 159; *id.* at 265 (the Latin); Mantilla, Vitoria, *supra* n.254, at 394 ("Vitoria did not mention when the causes for the killing of innocent human beings by human sacrifice ended. If the main cause for human sacrifice was the indigenous nations' worldviews, which led them to believe that it was good to kill innocent

himself knew at least of Aztec sacrifice and considered it a justification for war.[307] Oviedo and Hernán Cortés (1485–1547) were already regaling Europeans with bloody tales of cannibalism and human sacrifice.[308] Seventeenth-century Peruvian official Juan de Solórzano Pereira (1575–1655) (whom I discuss in Part 4.3.2 below) claimed that in marking transitions in imperial power, the Incans sacrificed "one thousand children, from four to ten years old" and "the wives of dead leaders were forced to be buried alive with their husbands."[309] Of course, child sacrifice was especially repulsive to Spaniards.[310]

In spite of this moral shock, Vitoria continues to endorse restraint and does not believe that all violations of natural rights should be punished by war. Perhaps thinking of Cajamarca,[311] he notes the possibility that "wars and massacres and spoliations will hinder rather than procure and further the conversion of the Indians."[312] And even a just war must be conducted proportionately.[313] Vitoria's Dominican student Juan de la Peña (1513–1565), who became a theology chair at Salamanca in his own right, honored this when he later wrote

---

persons for religious reasons, then changing this aspect of indigenous nations' beliefs required a very long time.").

307 *See* Mantilla, *Vitoria*, *supra* n.254, at 374, 381–82.

308 *See* Lantigua, *supra* n.42, at 152. Oviedo believed that God punished these crimes with widespread Indigenous death when Europeans arrived. *See id.* at 69.

309 Mantilla, *Vitoria*, *supra* n.254, at 357, 393–94.

310 *See* Muldoon, Americas, *supra* n.57, at 85. For more regarding Indigenous and European attitudes toward sacrifice, see Sacrifice and Conversion in the Early Modern Atlantic World (Maria Berbara ed., 2022).

311 Vitoria, De Indis, *supra* n.274, at 158 (without specifying: "I personally have no doubt that the Spaniards were bound to employ force and arms in order to continue their work … but I fear measures were adopted in excess of what is allowed by human and divine law."); *see also id.* at 264 (the Latin).

312 *Id.* at 158; *see also id.* at 264 (the Latin) ; *id.* at 179 ("Great attention … must be paid to the point already taken, namely, the obligation to see that greater evils do not arise out of the war than the war would avert.").

313 *See id.* at 171 ("As … the evils inflicted in war are all of a severe and atrocious character, such as slaughter and fire and devastation, it is not lawful for slight wrongs to pursue the authors of the wrongs with war, seeing that the degree of the punishment ought to correspond to the measure of the offence."), 182–83 ("Merely by way of avenging a wrong it is not always lawful to kill all the guilty. … For such conduct would not be for the public good, which is nevertheless the end and aim of both war and peace. … We ought, then, to take into account the nature of the wrong done by the enemy and of the damage they have caused and of their other offenses, and from that standpoint to move to our revenge and punishment, without any cruelty and inhumanity."); *but see* Mantilla, *Vitoria*, *supra* n.254, at 396 ("[T]he Spanish disproportionate use of force was a problem that Vitoria did not systematically address. … [E]ven a principle, which could have been considered universal and just, could also have had ethnocentric and unjust consequences in its implementation.").

that a war to protect people from sacrifice "certainly would be unjust" because more people "died in a few days [of] war than the ones that died in years of sacrifices."[314]

What is more, Vitoria foresees the restoration of equality when hostilities cease, with land, cities, and sometimes even sovereignty restored to the vanquished nation.[315] If occupation must continue, then it must be for the benefit of the locals and not the conquerors.[316] Having substituted natural law for papally sanctioned conquest, Vitoria tried to ensure that any war justified by humanitarian intervention would be limited by humanity.

4.2.1 Evaluating Vitoria and *Inter caetera*: an Influential Alternative

In meditating on law, peace, and Indigenous peoples, Vitoria kept in mind Spanish atrocities. His moral indignation remained as he rejected Alexander's authority to give Spain its empire. He derived from **natural law** a new, limited rationale for colonialism.

Vitoria's theories were very influential, and some writers have even incorrectly attributed to him the end of *Inter caetera*'s significance.[317] He did inspire the drafting of new laws that tried, and failed, to abolish the *encomiendas*.[318]

---

314 Juan de la Peña, De Bello contra Insulanos: Intervención de España en América: Escuela Española de La Paz, Segunda Generación, 1560–1585 p. 221 (Luciano Perena ed., 1982), *quoted in* Mantilla, *Tawantinsuyu*, *supra* n.162, at 326. Unfortunately, as noted above, Vitoria often failed to "carefully consider the implications" of his theories in "specific historical circumstances in which Spain could have imposed its will on indigenous nations," possibly because he lacked deep personal knowledge of Indigenous societies. Mantilla, *Vitoria*, *supra* n.254, at 370.

315 Vitoria, De Indis, *supra* n.274, at 185–87.

316 *See* Vitoria, De Potestate Civili, *supra* n.291, at 203; Miguel Anxo Peña González, *Derechos Humanos en la Escuela de Salamanca*, in Derechos Humanos en Europa 68 (José-Román Flecha Andres ed., 2009). Curiously, in spite of everything else Vitoria says and his own *converso* background, he anticipates that wars of extermination can sometimes be necessary, especially against unbelievers, because it is "useless ever to hope for a just peace on any terms" with them. Vitoria, De Indis, *supra* n.274, at 183; *see also id.* at 292 (the Latin). Precisely when he thought this was the case is unclear (he may have had in mind Christian-Muslim conflicts). In any event, he certainly did not apply this to the Americas.

317 *See* Lind, *supra* n.39, at 24.

318 *See Leyes Nuevas*, *reprinted in* Serna, *supra* n.140, at 345–61; Francisco Castilla Urbano, *The Debate of Valladolid (1550–1551): Background, Discussions, and Results of the Debate Between Juan Ginés de Sepúlveda and Bartolomé de Las Casas*, in Tellkamp, *supra* n.72, at 222 (trans. Carlos Diego Arenas Pacheco) ("After generating a huge conflict that led even to the murder of the viceroy of Peru, Blasco Núñez Vela [in 1546], the Spanish crown revoked the new legislation on the encomiendas, although their decline would prove to be unstoppable until their official disappearance in the eighteenth century."); Manuel Leal Lobón, *Antonio de Valdivieso*, Real Academia de la Historia, https://dbe.rah

And his intellectual heirs maintained his skepticism about the pope's temporal *dominium* over non-Christians, with some even reaching the conclusion that colonial conquest violated natural law.[319]

But Vitorian natural law did not completely displace *Inter caetera* as a matter of history. The bull continued to frame debate and even find an occasional champion.

4.3 *Later Imperialism (Late 1500s–Early 1600s): Vitorian Reformers and* Inter caetera*'s Continued Significance*

In the phase of colonialism that followed, new ideas existed alongside older questions about *Inter caetera*. Vitoria inspired reformers to protect Indigenous rights in Mexico and the Philippines. But in the following century, an important defense of *Inter caetera* was published. Alexander's words echoed even as other voices rose.

.es/biografias/4749/antonio-de-valdivieso (recounting the life of Antonio de Valdivieso, Dominican bishop of Nicaragua, assassinated in 1550 for attempting to implement the New Laws and so becoming "*el primer obispo mártir de América por defender los derechos humanos de los indios*" ("the first bishop-martyr of America [killed] for defending the human rights of the Indians")). Las Casas reacted to the repeal by "subjecting himself ... to a charge of high treason: he wrote twelve rules for confessors which declared the conquests illegal, denied absolution of sins until the penitent had performed restitution (to the Indians), and defied royal authority." Adorno, *supra* n.191, at 75.

319 *See, e.g.*, R. H. Helmholz, *Diego de Covarrubias v Leyva*, in Domingo & Martínez-Torrón, *supra* n.286, at 185–87; Lantigua, *supra* n.42, 193–250, 311–17 (discussing José de Acosta (1539–1600), Melchor Cano, and Juan de la Peña (1513–1565)); Pagden, *Dispossessing*, *supra* n.72, at 88–90, 92–95 (discussing Cano and Peña). Acosta turned the Empire's humanitarian rationales against it: "Hardly, has there ever been committed so many and so huge crimes by one barbarian and ferocious people ... as by those defenders of natural law, and by the propagators of the Christian faith"—the colonizers. Mantilla, *Tawantinsuyu*, *supra* n.162, at 309–10 (*quoting* José de Acosta, De Procuranda Indorum Salute: Pacificación y Colonización 281 (Luciano Perena ed., Consejo Superior de Investigaciones Científicas 1984) (1588)). But Acosta, whose life approached colonization's third century, thought that "despite [colonization's] irrational foundation, [it] must be continued in the name of a more transcendent purpose." Ivonne del Valle, *José de Acosta: Colonial Regimes for a Globalized Christian World*, in Coloniality, Religion, and the Law in the Early Iberian World 20–21 (Santa Arias & Raúl Marrero-Fente eds., 2014); *cf.* McAlister, *supra* n.116, at 302 ("[B]y the end of Philip[II]'s reign [in 1598], society in the Indies no longer consisted of a handful of European intruders lording it over a seemingly inexhaustible Indian population through native intermediaries and institutions. It had become much more complex and was assuming distinctively Hispanic American qualities."); J. Michelle Molina, *Fluid Indigeneity: Indians, Catholicism, and Spanish Law in the Mutable Americas*, The Immanent Frame, July 12, 2017, https://tif.ssrc.org/2017/07/12/fluid-indigeneity/ (criticizing "a seemingly constant effort—whether colonial or scholarly—to draw boundaries that would attempt to conceptually 'fix' the settler/indigenous divide, a divide that projects each as a distinct monoculture").

4.3.1 Zumárraga (Mid-1500s) and Salazar (Late 1500s): Vitorian Moderation

Just as Montesinos's seeds bore fruit across the Atlantic at Salamanca, so did Vitoria's words reach the colonies in return. His natural-law ideas led bishops on both sides of an ocean—this time, the Pacific—to fight for Indigenous rights. Juan de Zumárraga (*c.*1468–1548), first bishop of Mexico City, defended Indians against slavery and wars of conquest using Vitorian ideas.[320] Where Vitoria lacked a deep awareness of ground conditions,[321] Zumárraga showed that an attentive Christian could take from him plenty of reasons to oppose abuses.[322] Even though Zumárraga did not reject colonization altogether, he said that *Inter caetera*'s evangelizing purpose had been "replaced by robbery, thus perverting and turning into an unjust cause the presence of the Spaniards in America."[323]

On the other side of the globe, the first bishop of Manila, the Dominican Domingo de Salazar (*c.*1512–1594), had been Vitoria's student and a veteran of the American colonies.[324] He initially applied Vitoria's logic to find a just cause for war with China based on Christian preachers being refused entry. But like Zumárraga, he followed facts. When he realized that the Chinese were hostile to missionaries only because they feared conquest, he called for peace and praised Chinese learning.[325] Vitoria gave him reasons to oppose colonial expansion.

---

320 *See* Mauricio Beuchot, *The Philosophical Discussion of the Legitimacy of the Conquest of Mexico in the Sixteenth Century*, in White, *supra* n.198 (Concepción Abellán trans.). Zumárraga is also remembered as a key figure in accounts of the Marian apparition to St. Juan Diego at Guadalupe, which hagiography identifies as central to Aztec conversions. *See* Ambrose Mong, *Our Lady of Guadalupe: Model of Inculturation*, 18 Int'l J. Stud. Christian Church 67, 75–78, 81–82 (2018) (detailing the traditional account and modern historical critiques). However, he also organized the destruction of Indigenous literature. *See* Adorno, *supra* n.191, at 212. For more regarding Zumárraga, see Pedro Borges Morán, *Juan de Zumárraga*, Diccionario Biográfico Electrónico, https://dbe.rah.es/biografias/6774/juan-de-zumarraga.

321 *See* discussion *supra* at nn.299–300.

322 *See* Beuchot, *supra* n.320, at 35.

323 *See id.* at 33–34. Similarly, Vasco de Quiroga [1477/78–1565], bishop of Michoacán, followed Vitoria in thinking that the hostility of Indigenous rulers to Christian preaching justified war, but he also opposed conquest and enslavement, proposed letting Indian sovereigns rule under Spanish oversight, and worked to preserve Indigenous languages. *See id.* at 36–38; *Vasco de Quiroga*, Britannica, https://www.britannica.com/biography/Vasco-de-Quiroga.

324 *See* Cervera, *supra* n.167, at 14–16. Cervera also discusses Salamanca-educated Martín de Rada (1533–1578), the Augustinian prior in Manila and an opponent of *encomiendas*. *See id.* at 7.

325 *See id.* at 17–18.

Interestingly, though, Spanish threats to China echoed the *Requerimiento*. The Crown believed it should bring the Chinese to understand their "obligation" to serve.[326] Likewise, Salazar's last fight, in the 1590s, concerned an issue relevant to Vitoria and *Inter caetera*. He fought Spanish taxation of those Filipinos "who had never heard about Christ" as "robbery" because colonization was justified only as a means of evangelization.[327] He went all the way to Madrid to protest to King Philip II (r. 1556–1598). His protests were initially unsuccessful, but Philip ordered restitution to Indigenous non-Christians after Salazar's death.[328]

Vitorian natural law gave new life to reform efforts on behalf of Indigenous peoples. But it did not displace entirely *Inter caetera*. In fact, until the late 1700s—when Spain's American colonies were near to declaring independence—Alexander's bull was "represented in the historiography of the Spanish empire as a donation" of much of the world.[329] It was "the only explanation for the Spanish presence in America" offered by Antonio de Herrera in his 1601–15 royal histories.[330] It also received a detailed new analysis several years later.

4.3.2 Solórzano (1626): Relying on *Inter caetera* Once More

There was an interim when *Inter caetera* was cited less due to papal-imperial tensions and the predominance of natural-law thought.[331] But at least one important treatment had yet to be written: that of Solórzano, the Peruvian official.[332] He published a lengthy defense of Spanish control of the New World in 1626.[333] As he canvasses various religious and legal rationales, *Inter caetera* is a constant touchstone.[334] He champions Alexander's authority to punish infidels by subjecting them to Castile.

326 *Id.* at 10 (translation mine).

327 *Id.* at 19.

328 *See id.* at 19–20.

329 Pagden, Lords, *supra* n.44, at 32; *see also* Barrientos, *supra* n.5, at 68, 72, 81 *et seq.* (quoting sources from the second half of the sixteenth century all the way to 1743).

330 Pagden, Lords, *supra* n.44, at 48.

331 *See id.* at 47.

332 *See id.* at 48–49.

333 By this point, the Spanish Empire was so entrenched in the Americas that colonists and Indians were becoming, in Solórzano's words, "one religion and republic." 3 Juan de Solórzano Pereira, De Indiarum Iure: De Retentione Indiarum 356 (Carlos Baciero ed., Consejo Superior de Investigaciones Científicas 1994) (1626) [hereinafter Retentione]; *see also* McAlister, *supra* n.116, at 302. Solórzano wanted it to have one language, too, calling for a ban on Indigenous tongues. *See* Adorno, *supra* n.191, at 213.

334 Notably, Solórzano accepts a doctrine of discovery like that criticized by modern activists. *See* 2 Juan de Solórzano Pereira, De Indiarum Iure: De Acquisitione Indiarum (Cap. 1–15) 174 (Carlos Baciero ed., Consejo Superior de Investigaciones Científicas 1999) (1626)

Starting with explicitly religious arguments, Solórzano notes that some believe that the Holy Spirit led Alexander to assign the West Indies to Castile and Portugal.[335] He even considers the possibility that God directly handed over the colonies, citing various miracles.[336] Solórzano mentions Hostiensis's opinion regarding infidel *dominium* as well as Innocent's opposing view.[337] While accepting Innocent's position in the abstract, he attempts a synthesis, concluding that the pope can transfer infidels' *dominium* to Christians for a just reason.[338] In fact, he reaches Hostiensis's conclusion by way of Innocent's reasoning: precisely because infidel *dominium* arises through natural reason and not divine grace, it can be "dissolved."[339] Just causes for doing so include protecting missionaries and aiding evangelization.[340] Loss of *dominium* for these reasons is not punishment, but simply a matter of higher goods intervening

---

[hereinafter Acquisitione]. He also attributes to Spain a civilizing mission. *See id.* at 320; *see also* M. C. Mirow, *Juan Solórzano Pereira*, in Domingo & Martínez-Torrón, *supra* n.286, at 251 (noting that he deems Indians *miserabilis personae*—people in need of benevolent care, like orphans and widows); Nancy Buenger, *Equitable Justice in Progressive Chicago and the Philippines*, in At Home and Abroad: The Politics of American Religion 54 (Elizabeth Shakman Hurd & Winnifred Fallers Sullivan eds., 2021) (discussing this category's canonical history).

335 See Solórzano, Acquisitione, supra n.334, at 96 (naming Giovanni Botero and Rutilio Benzoni).

336 *See id.* at 54–85, 116–73.

337 *See id.* at 348–81.

338 *See id.* at 386 ("[P]lanius pleniusque est verum quidem esse dominium rerum et iurisdictionis propter infidelitatem nequaquam excludi posse, tamen Romanum Pontificem ex potestate sibi a Christo communicata illud ab infidelibus ad fideles ex iusta causa transferre ...." ["It is evidently true that that this *dominium* over goods and jurisdiction cannot be excluded due to infidelity, but the Roman Pontiff, from the power communicated to him by Christ, can transfer it from infidels to believers for a just cause"]).

339 *Id.* at 386; *see also id.* at 396 (acknowledging compatibility of his judgment with Hostiensis's).

Muldoon characterizes Solórzano as accepting global papal dominium. *See* Muldoon, Americas, *supra* n.57, at 117–22, 125–28. This is true in a sense; M. C. Mirow observes that Solórzano follows St. Robert Cardinal Bellarmine's distinction between direct and indirect papal temporal power. *See* Mirow, *supra* n.334, at 247; Robert Bellarmine, On Temporal and Spiritual Authority (Stefania Turino ed., Liberty Fund 2012).

Intriguingly, Solórzano says that Alexander partly rehabilitated Hostiensis in commentaries on the Decretals and *Summa* (presumably, Hostiensis's work of that name), by way of references to Catellianus Cotta (1512–1553) and Valentin Wilhelm Forster (1530–1608). *See* Solórzano, Acquisitione, *supra* n.334, at 352, 366; entries for "Valentinus Forster" and "Catellianus Cotta," Bio-Bibliographical Guide to Medieval and Early Modern Jurists, https://amesfoundation.law.harvard.edu/BioBibCanonists/index.php. I have not found commentaries fitting his description.

340 *See* Solórzano, Acquisitione, *supra* n.334, at 386.

against lower ones.[341] Any such intervention "proceeds from the divine will," which "is declared by the popes."[342]

Solórzano also writes that as Christ's vicar, the pope "can punish in imitation of God" and compel non-Christians to observe natural law.[343] He is at least confident that the pope can authorize intervention, though noting as well the opinion that natural law authorizes war against idolatry that injures innocent people (such as human sacrifice).[344] While the pope lacks jurisdiction over infidels, he can "vindicate natural justice and defend the innocent."[345]

That *Inter caetera* authorized Castile to execute such justice in the Americas is a natural conclusion. Solórzano does say that Alexander "assigned" the "conquest" of the New World to Castile and "conceded" to it "perpetual" possession of the continents.[346] Such jurisdiction inheres in the authorization to evangelize, as spiritual power brings with it everything necessary for salvation; *dominium* also aided Castile instrumentally in executing its mission.[347] Next, he cautiously argues that even if the bull were not "as clear as it is," its purposes could not be achieved without civil power, so it has to be interpreted as giving it.[348] Solórzano also praises Isabella and Ferdinand's piety in seeking a papal blessing, asserting that this should satisfy those who condition conquest on papal permission.[349]

341 *See id.* at 394 (noting that "neminem regulaliter sine culpa puniri aut re sua privari debere" ["no one should without fault be punished or deprived of his private possession"] and "nisi subsit causa, non est aliquis puniendus" ["no one without cause is punished"], but then discussing "causae et rationes intervenient" [intervening causes and reasons]).

342 *Id.* at 394–96.

343 *Id.* at 466.

344 *See id.* at 468; *id.* at 560. He notes the need to warn infidels and give them a choice, recalling the *Requerimiento* (which had fallen out of use). *See* Hanke, Struggle, *supra* n.151, at 112, 131.

345 Solórzano, Acquisitione, *supra* n.334, at 564.

346 Solórzano, Retentione, *supra* n.333, at 218.

347 *Id.* at 218–20. Similarly, he defends the Spanish record of spreading Catholicism and bettering Indigenous lives, which he identifies as Alexander's highest priorities. *See id.* at 220–22, 404.

348 *Id.* at 224. For a description of the earlier, similar theory of the Mexican Augustinian Alonso de la Veracruz (1507–1584), *see* Egío, *supra* n.202, at 46–47. Felipe Castañeda suggests that for Solórzano, the meaning of *Inter caetera* is revealed by the events subsequent to its issuance. *See* Castañeda, *supra* n.207, at 278 ("It is events that provide an indicator of the contents of the Bull rather than the Bull being an ultimate reference point used to justify these events ...."). I see this as secondary to Solórzano's insistence that the bull clearly authorized the conquests, but Castañeda's point is well-taken. Solórzano was more interested in bolstering the Empire by all arguable means than in asserting one logical chain of justification.

349 *See* Solórzano, Retentione, *supra* n.333, at 230.

But then, he starts to hedge. In rejecting papal oversight of the colonies, he suggests that *others* could see the bull as "superfluous" because a sovereign need not ask the pope for what the law already allows.[350] Were one to *hypothetically* accept this reading, then *Inter caetera* merely offered Castile's right of conquest "security and corroboration."[351] And consulting with the pope, together with "the most prudent and learned men," gave the royals firm ground for thinking that colonization was just.[352] Thus, Castile acted in good faith at the outset and can hold onto the territory it has long claimed (a legal doctrine known as "prescription").[353]

Has Solórzano lost his papalist nerve? Or is he simply raising alternative justifications? Possibly the latter. He proceeds to tentatively defend *Inter caetera*'s assignment of navigation rights on the basis that many say the pope has worldwide political power.[354] He also asserts papal authority to set Christian sovereigns over newly converted Indigenous peoples.[355]

He may be softening his claims about papal power, or raising them selectively, because he is an imperial official. He wants to use *Inter caetera* to defend Spanish claims without undermining them. For instance, against the opinion of Jean Bodin (1529/30–1596), he contends that Spain is not a papal vassal in the colonies.[356] He also rejects any active role for the Papacy in supervising the colonies, and any papal authority to transfer them to another power.[357]

Did Solórzano's counterpoise succeed? He did earn respect at home.[358] But in 1647, the Papacy censored his work because of its limited view of ecclesiastical

350 *Id.* at 230–32. Solórzano denies that he means to lessen *Inter caetera*'s significance, a caveat Castañeda does not mention. *See* Castañeda, *supra* n.348, at 278 ("[T]he support of the Pope confirmed the legitimacy of the cause but does not appear to have established itself as a necessary condition.").

351 Solórzano, Retentione, *supra* n.333, at 234.

352 *Id.* at 260; *see also id.* at 266.

353 *See id.* at 272. Pagden incorrectly claims that Solórzano relies only on prescription. *See* Pagden, *Dispossessing*, *supra* n.72, at 97.

354 *See* Solórzano, Retentione, *supra* n.333, at 292; *see also id.* at 230 (asserting also papal authority to coordinate the global Church).

355 *See id.* at 356.

356 *See id.* at 226–28. For historiographical debate regarding the papal-vassal theory, see García Gallo, *supra* n.5, at 684–93.

357 *See* Muldoon, Americas, *supra* n.57, at 163; Pagden, Lords, *supra* n.44, at 47 ("It is not surprising, given the uneasy relations between the Papacy and ... Philip II, that few Spaniards should have wished to uphold the Papacy's old claim to be the ultimate arbiter in international disputes."). Relatedly, Spain controlled ecclesiastical appointments within the colonies. *See* Stogre, *supra* n.86, at 68; Ramón Valdivia Giménez, Llamado a La Misión Pacífica: La Dimensión Religiosa de la Libertad en Bartolomé de Las Casas 125–26 (2010).

358 *See generally* Mirow, *supra* n.334.

authority.[359] Solórzano defended the rights of the Spanish Empire based on the Holy Spirit, law, and *Inter caetera*. Still, the bull held significance for him due to his exalted notion of papal power—at least in initiating conquest, if not in guiding it. For him, no less than for the first *conquistadores*, Spain received its colonies from Alexander's hand.

4.3.3 Evaluating Late Interpretations of *Inter caetera*: Signs of Vitality

Zumárraga and Salazar applied Vitoria's natural-law concepts to their colonial settings and advocated for Indigenous rights. To them, *Inter caetera* could not justify exploitation (and at least for Zumárraga, gave reasons to oppose it). But the intellectual climate had not become entirely inhospitable to the bull. After both of these bishops died, there was **Solórzano**, tracing Spain's empire right back to Alexander. As Pagden wrote, the bull was no "dead letter."[360]

4.4 *Evaluating the Spanish Debates around* Inter caetera: *a Flexible Bull*

Inter caetera was debated by a wide range of people in many places over a long period of time. The disputes follow a threefold pattern: taken at face value, *Inter caetera* is cited as a basis for conquest. Protest erupts. Then, Alexander's words receive a refining interpretation reaffirming their value for empire. This cycle repeats twice over the time period we have considered, with Palacios Rubios as the connecting link:

> Citation (early invaders) → protest (Montesinos) → refinement (Palacios Rubios)
> Citation (Palacios Rubios) → protest (Vitoria) → refinement (Solórzano)

Inter caetera is relished. Rejected. And restored.

I do not mean to suggest any hidden structures of history, but merely to observe that *Inter caetera*'s meaning evolved, with each new interpretation offering new promises and causing new problems. Contrary to what some modern Catholic apologists have suggested, though, it was never a nonentity. It always mattered, even if the reasons why changed.

Inter caetera proved flexible throughout these debates. It did not depend on natural law, but it could exist alongside it. Advocates for both war and moderation could cite it. That adaptability lessened the need to contest it directly, although challenges were sometimes raised, too.

359 *See* Muldoon, Americas, *supra* n.57, at 163.
360 Pagden, Lords, *supra* n.44, at 48.

Just how many meanings could the bull sustain? That is the question posed by Las Casas. He did not reject *Inter caetera*; he embraced it even more radically than Solórzano. But he did not embrace empire; he rejected it even more radically than Vitoria.

5 *Inter caetera* Inverted: Las Casas (Mid-1500s)

Las Casas deserves consideration out of chronological order because his interpretation of *Inter caetera* is radically **inverted** vis-à-vis any other. The Hispaniola convert found in *Inter caetera* no justification for conquest, only reasons to defend Indigenous rights—in the end, even political independence. Years before he arrived at this most radical conclusion, he debated a leading proponent of forcible colonization. I start by discussing the later Las Casas, then go back to peruse his radical reading of the bull, before noting his real-world impact.

Elena Cirkovic has written that imperialist violence became so submerged into the colonial psyche that "any rebellion" was seen as violating "the universal legal order."[361] This was certainly many Spaniards' evaluation of Incan resistance following Atahuallpa's 1533 murder.[362] Not Las Casas. In 1561, Philip II tried to negotiate the sale of the American *encomiendas*.[363] In response, Dominican friar Domingo de Santo Tomás organized Indigenous Peruvian nobles (*kurakas*) "who proposed the direct subordination of all the encomiendas to the Crown instead and committed to pay a price that surpassed the offer of the encomenderos."[364] Las Casas—who had been consecrated bishop of Chiapa in 1543—used the occasion (which ended with the status quo being maintained) to defend the right of Incans to wage war against the Empire.[365] He interpreted *Inter caetera* as conditioning Castile's assumption

---

361 Elena Cirkovic, *Self-Determination and Indigenous Peoples in International Law*, 31 Am. Indian L. Rev. 375, 378 (2006), *quoted in* Mantilla, Tawantinsuyu, *supra* n.162, at 329.

362 *See* Mantilla, *Tawantinsuyu*, *supra* n.162, at 323–26.

363 *See* Victor Zorrilla, *Just War in Las Casas's* Tratado de las Doce Dudas, in Bartolomé de Las Casas, O.P.: History, Philosophy, and Theology in the Age of European Expansion 252 (David Thomas Orique O.P. & Rady Roldán-Figueroa eds., 2019); Adorno, *supra* n.191, at 85 ("In 1554–1555, the encomenderos of Peru presented the prospective king Philip II with a remarkable offer: They would buy the perpetual rights to the use of the lands and services of the native peoples of Peru from the king of Spain.").

364 Zorrilla, *supra* n.363, at 252; Adorno, *supra* n.191, at 85.

365 *See* Zorrilla, *supra* n.363, at 253; Adorno, *supra* n.191, at 86; David Orique O.P., *Bartolomé de Las Casas (1484–1566): A* Brevísima *Biographical Sketch*, 85–86 INTI 32, 38 (2017).

of sovereignty on Indian consent.[366] Because Castile never received it, the Indians "acquired the right to wage war against the Spaniards the moment the latter burst into their lands, especially when they apprehended King Atahualpa."[367] Incans could fight "to regain their liberty, their kingdoms and their stolen treasures, as well as reinstating the rule of the legitimate heirs to Atahualpa and the rest of the dispossessed rulers."[368] They could even retaliate against European injustices.[369] As for the colonists? They were aggressors who had no right to defend themselves, but should instead "flee or hide."[370]

The seeds of Las Casas's root-and-branch rejection of colonization, sown by Montesinos, had begun to flower a decade earlier in the famous 1550–51 *junta* at Valladolid.[371] Charles V convened this dispute between Las Casas and Juan

---

366 *See* Zorrilla, *supra* n.363, at 254.

367 *Id.* at 254–55.

368 *Id.* at 255.

369 *See id.* at 256. Las Casas also argued that because the *conquistas* were private endeavors, soldiers bore personal guilt for participating in them. *See id.* at 257.

370 *Quoted in* Lantigua, *supra* n.42, at 310. By this point, Las Casas had gone beyond calling for reform. *See* Marks, *supra* n.177, at 36–37 ("He lost interest in the protectorate system with Spain pre-eminent, which he had earlier envisaged, and increasingly he simply equated the sovereignties of Spain and the Indian caciques."). Newcomb overlooks this. *See* Newcomb, *Evidence*, *supra* n.19, at 312–13 ("Even Fray Bartolomé de Las Casas ... could do no more than to create a theory of empire in which Indians were deemed to be subjects of the Spanish Crown."). Williams Jr., the Lumbee legal scholar, rightly credits Las Casas with rejecting "European cultural hegemony over the Indian" and defending Indigenous political freedom. Robert A. Williams Jr., *The Medieval and Renaissance Origins of the Status of the American Indian in Western Legal Thought*, 57 S. Calif. L. Rev. 1, 84, 98 (1983), *quoted in Marks*, *supra* n.177, at 47–48.

371 Las Casas's belief that God lovingly made each human being was his ultimate foundation. *See* Las Casas, Defense, *supra* n.278, at 28 ("[T]he Creator of every being has not so despised these peoples of the New World that he willed them to lack reason and made them like brute animals, so that they should be called barbarians, savages, wild men, and brutes, as they [Sepúlveda and so on] think or imagine."); Terence Sweeney, *Bartolomé de las Casas on the Naturalness of Evangelization*, Church Life J., Oct. 27, 2022, https://churchlifejournal.nd.edu/articles/bartolome-de-las-casas-on-the-naturalness-of-evangelization/.

An important caveat, though: in the late 1510s, Las Casas proposed replacing the *encomiendas* with European and African slaves. He assumed that such people were captives taken in just wars. "By 1546, however, the rise of the sugar economy based in racialized slavery brought Las Casas to the conclusion that such an assumption was no longer tenable, and he therefore repudiated his earlier position." Darryl Li, *Genres of Universalism: Reading Race into International Law, with Help from Sylvia Winter*, 67 UCLA L. Rev. 1686, 1708–11, 1714 (2021); *see also* Clayton & Lantigua, *supra* n.128, at 49–51 (quoting Las Casas, writing of himself in the third person: "He was not certain that his ignorance and his good intentions would excuse him before the judgment of God."); Adorno, *supra* n.191, at 64 ("Contrary to popular opinion, Las Casas was not the originator of African slavery in the

Ginés de Sepúlveda (1489–1573), a leading humanist and proponent of forceful colonization.[372] Charles did so out of conscientious concern about colonization, ordering officials to pause conquest until after the *junta* concluded (an order put into effect in New Granada, the Paraguayan Chaco, and Costa Rica).[373] The *junta* was meant to generate new perspectives that might give Charles an acceptable way forward.[374]

Las Casas and Sepúlveda debated before fourteen jurists and theologians.[375] Sepúlveda followed Innocent in defending indirect coercion.[376] Like Palacios Rubios before him (and von der Heydte centuries later), Sepúlveda saw *Inter caetera* as anticipating that political domination would aid evangelization.[377] He also identified the law of nations as supporting "a right of superior peoples

---

Indies. It had begun within the first decade of Columbus's arrival in America."); *id.* at 67 (identifying Las Casas's turning point as becoming aware that the papal bulls sanctioning Portuguese exploits in West Africa were what led to enslavement). It is tragic that this foremost champion of Indian rights supported for a time the enslavement of another race. It is also admirable that he repented of this at a time when so few other Europeans did. *See* Kenneth Pennington, *Bartolomé de Las Casas*, in Domingo & Martínez-Torrón, *supra* n.286, at 111. Like Paz and Vitoria, Las Casas's personal background may have contributed to his empathy; he, too, may have been a *converso*. *See* Orique, *supra* n.180, at 52. At the very least, he had an Indian page during his student years, and upon arriving in the Americas, he "entered into family-type relations with his former page's family." Marks, *supra* n.177, at 20.

372 *See* Marks, *supra* n.177, at 22.

373 *See* Urbano, *supra* n.318, at 244; Hanke, Struggle, *supra* n.151, at 116–17 ("[T]he Council of the Indies ... advised the King that the dangers both to the bodies of the Indians and to the King's conscience which the conquests incurred were so great that no new expeditions ought to be licensed without his express permission and that of the Council. Moreover, concluded the Council, a meeting of theologians and jurists was needed ...."). The *junta* also occurred as Charles sought power against colonial and Church officials. *See* Urbano, *supra* n.318, at 244, 246–47 (noting that after the *junta*, Madrid took full power over authorizing new excursions—a process that ultimately led to Indians being released from the *encomiendas* and made direct tributaries of the Crown, and religious orders being sidelined). Spain's monarchy was long cast as a vindicator of popular rights against abusive local officials. For instance, in 1619, famed Spanish playwright Lope Félix de Vega Carpio published *Fuenteovejuna*, in which a town collectively accepts guilt for assassinating a corrupt official and is then exonerated by Isabella and Ferdinand. *See* Roberto González Echevarría, *Introduction to* Lope de Vega, Fuenteovejuna *xvii–xviii* (G. J. Racz trans., Yale Univ. Press 2010) (1619).

374 *See* Benjamin Hill, *Domingo de Soto*, in Domingo & Martínez-Torrón, *supra* n.286, at 145.

375 *See* Marks, *supra* n.177, at 22.

376 *See* Urbano, *supra* n.318, at 231; Lantigua, *supra* n.42, at 170. Urbano explores differences between the men's oral presentations and the edited versions of their arguments that survive today. *See* Urbano, *supra* n.318, at 229.

377 *See id.* at 238, 240–41; von der Heydte, *supra* n.115, at 452, 457–58.

to enforce natural law," including by bettering inferior societies through political domination.[378] The *Requerimiento* reasonably informed Indigenous peoples of these norms and gave them a chance to deliberate, so resistance to it justified war against depravities like human sacrifice.[379]

Sepúlveda understood *Inter caetera* as confirming this natural right, rather than being strictly necessary.[380] But he still prioritized the bull enough to write a work tellingly entitled: "Against those who depreciate or contradict the bull and decree of Pope Alexander VI which gives the Catholic Kings and their successors authority to conquer the Indies and subject those barbarians, and by this means convert them to the Christian religion and submit them to their empire and jurisdiction."[381]

Whom did he mean? Las Casas. Of course, the bishop did not see himself as rejecting *Inter caetera*, but merely contextualizing it. "What serious man has

---

378 Lantigua, *supra* n.42, at 181. Urbano rightly notes that Sepúlveda did not characterize Indians as Aristotle's natural slaves (something he is frequently accused of, including by Las Casas). *See* Urbano, *supra* n.318, at 231–32, 237–38. Scottish scholar John Mair of the University of Paris (*c.*1469–1550) held this opinion. *See* Lantigua, *supra* n.42, at 77–81. But Sepúlveda said that the Spanish should only "subjugate [Indigenous peoples] without committing any acts of injustice against them." *Quoted in id.* at 184. This may sound like a distinction without a difference, but it meant some personal liberty and property rights, and even progressive increases in political rights as Indians became more developed—although Sepúlveda disavowed knowing whether they would ever equal Europeans. *See* Avira & Cruz, *supra* n.197, at 103–04, 107.

379 Lantigua, *supra* n.42, at 183; *see also* Juan Ginés de Sepúlveda, Tratado sobre Las Justas Causas de la Guerra Contra los Indios 84 (Manuel García-Pelayo ed., Fondo De Cultura Económica 1941). Sepúlveda did emphasize restraint in war and thought only limited force would be necessary to overcome Indian resistance. *See* Eduardo Andújar, *Bartolomé de las Casas and Juan Ginés de Sepúlveda: Moral Theology versus Political Philosophy*, in White, *supra* n.197, at 85–86; Avira & Cruz, *supra* n.197, at 101.

Sepúlveda and Las Casas widely diverged in estimating the number of Indigenous human sacrifices. *See* Urbano, *supra* n.318, at 236–37 (noting that Sepúlveda estimated 20,000 annually, while Las Casas doubted that there were even fifty). Historian Caroline Dodds Pennock has noted that we "lack the sources which would permit us to enter the statistical debate with any confidence." Caroline Dodds Pennock, *Mass Murder or Religious Homicide? Rethinking Human Sacrifice and Interpersonal Violence in Aztec Society*, 37 Hist. Soc. Rsch. (Köln) 276, 278 (2012). But surveying early *conquistador* accounts of skull racks near the main temple in the Aztec capital of Tenochtitlan, which may not be altogether reliable, she very tentatively concludes that the number was much closer to Sepúlveda's: "Certainly an annual number of victims of 1,000–20,000 remains in line with the limited evidence … suggesting a possible figure of 400–8,000 sacrifices per 100,000 population per year [at that one key site]." *Id.* at 284.

380 *See* Lantigua, *supra* n.42, at 183.

381 Hanke, Struggle, *supra* n.151, at 119.

ever taken up the pen without an exact knowledge of the facts and the law?" he asks.[382] And know the law he does.[383] He relies on legal rules to reinterpret *Inter caetera*'s text because, according to one such norm, "the will of a ruler is always to be judged in conformity with the law."[384] Other fundamental rules concern jurisdiction. Las Casas reads canon law as limiting the Church's non-consensual jurisdiction over non-Christians.[385] Only within Christian realms can believers punish infidels' sins (and the same holds true in the inverse, he takes care to note).[386] What is more, the Church does not even punish the non-Christianity of Jews and Muslims living within Christendom; much less so can it punish "idolaters who inhabit an immense portion of the earth, which was unheard of in previous centuries, who have never been subjects of either the Church or her members, and who have not even known what the Church is."[387] Nor can it punish the less serious (because derivative of unbelief in Christianity) sin of idolatry.[388] Infidels living beyond Christendom are only

382 Las Casas, Defense, *supra* n.278, at 339. Las Casas was not Sepúlveda's only contemporary critic. His first major publication on colonization was censured by the Council of the Indies and, according to Las Casas, did not impress the ecumenical Council of Trent (1545–63). *See* Urbano, *supra* n.318, at 223. On the other hand, after Valladolid, Mexico City's colonial government tried to give Sepúlveda "up to two hundred pesos of gold in jewels and clothing." *Id.* at 243.

383 Las Casas marshals so many Roman, canonical, and feudal legal authorities that historian Kenneth Pennington concludes that he could not have been a mere dilettante. *See* Pennington, *supra* n.371, at 100–01. For a contrary opinion, see Valdivia Jiménez, *supra* n.209, at 172, 184 ("[A]ll Las Casas knew about law (in addition to his [confirmed] study of canon law) consisted mainly in what he learned from ... Palacios Rubios, from [Paz], and from his connections first with the court of Ferdinand, and then with the court of the Regent Cisneros. * * * * [F]riar Reginaldo de Montesinos gave Las Casas a wider knowledge of legal formulations that originated in the universities of Valladolid and Salamanca ...."); *but see id.* at 192 (observing that Las Casas had access to more legal materials and experts toward the end of 1552).

384 Las Casas, Defense, *supra* n.278, at 349; *see also id.* n.1 (citing to Gratian and the Decretals); Bartolomé de Las Casas, Apologia Fratris Bartholomaei a Casaus adversus Genesium Sepulvedam 244, *available at* https://gallica.bnf.fr/ark:/12148/btv1b9080777g.image [hereinafter "Apologia"] (translations from this are mine). Regarding manuscript difficulties, which are why I cite several versions, see *Introduction to* Las Casas, Defense, *supra* n.278, at *xiv–xvi*.

385 Las Casas, Defense, *supra* n.278, at 61; Valdivia Jiménez, *supra* n.209, at 190.

386 *See* Las Casas, Defense, *supra* n.278, at 54.

387 *Id.* at 79.

388 *See id.* at 77. Las Casas did accept Church coercion of Christians. *See id.* at 68 (allowing for the destruction of idols retained by converts).

subject to Christian jurisdiction potentially.[389] Recalling Innocent, Las Casas reasserts that the pope has "care of the men of the whole world," but only "to invite and attract pagans to the Catholic faith or protect and strengthen them in the truths of the faith."[390]

Relying on his understanding of jurisdiction and another legal rule against interpreting documents in a way that leads to "inhumanity or absurdity,"[391] Las Casas stunningly criticizes Innocent for sanctioning religious wars against idolatry: "With all due respect to such a great doctor, we say that if his opinion has to be taken without distinctions it is subject to many contrary arguments."[392] Las Casas also relies on Aquinas's and Paz's doctrine of invincible ignorance to ethically excuse non-Christians for many religious crimes (not just unbelief).[393] Like Vitoria, Las Casas says that miracles, preaching, and good Christian living are the way to make Christianity believable—to make ignorance vincible.[394] But he notes both an absence of miracles and the devastation, pillaging, and murder committed by Christian colonizers.[395] He thus concludes that "a great

---

389 *Id.* at 59; *see also* Bartolomé de Las Casas et al., Una Disputa, o Controversia, entre el Casas o Lacaus obispo q fue dela las Indias parte dela nueva Espa. 16 (Sebastian Trugillo, 1552), Gale: Sabin Americana [hereinafter Disputa] (noting that all are subject to Christ "en potencia/empero no en actu," so there is no jurisdiction over them until they are "detro dela yglia: cuya puerta y entrada es por la fee" ["inside of the Church, whose door and entrance is through faith"]); Las Casas, Defense, *supra* n.278, at 56 ("[A]ll peoples of the earth are his [Christ's] subjects by the authority and power over every creature which he has received, not only as God but also as man, from the Eternal Father. Yet, despite this, not all of them are actually or effectively subject to him, not even as regards the exercise of his power."); *id.* at 79–80 ("[N]o ruler, whether king or emperor, nor anyone else, can exercise jurisdiction beyond his borders .... [The sacraments] are the borders or walls by which the Church is surrounded.").

390 Las Casas, Defense, *supra* n.278, at 97.

391 *Id.* at 123–24.

392 *Id.* at 126.

393 *See id.* at 127–28; *see also id.* at 233 (accepting even human sacrifice as logically compatible with natural reason); Hanke, Mankind, *supra* n.305, at 94 ("... Las Casas recognized the good faith of the pagan in his religion ...."). Las Casas provides a colorful example drawn from his pastoral experience: "If ... pagans speak blasphemously about the Christian religion not out of contempt and hatred of religion but out of anger toward Christians by whom they have been maltreated and injured, that is, with lawful cause, such persons are not blasphemous. Such is the case of the Indians of Jalisco, where, in order to ridicule priests and Christians, the Indians would lift a little cake [likely a tortilla] over their heads with both hands in imitation of the practice of Christian priests [in consecrating the Eucharist] ...." Las Casas, Defense, *supra* n.278, at 165; *Translator's commentary to id.* at 377.

394 *See* Las Casas, Defense, *supra* n.278, at 134.

395 *See id.* at 136.

many unbelievers are excused from accepting the faith for a long time and perhaps for their whole lifetime."[396]

Even more radically, Las Casas rejects indirect coercion, again appealing to first principles: "they who teach that these gentlest of sheep must be tamed by ravening wolves in a savage war before they are to be fed with the word of God are wrong."[397] As for infidels who sin against natural law, it "has its defenders and guardians everywhere," including their own sovereigns, who draw their authority from natural law, the law of nations, and divine law.[398] The Church can war against these non-believers only if they "defile Christian lands with their filth or assail [Christians] personally."[399]

What about the right to evangelize? Las Casas does accept papal punishment of those who kill or sacrifice innocent people who could convert, oppress Christian subjects, or prevent voluntary conversions.[400] But even this should be sparing due to the evils and excesses inherent in war (which Las Casas had chronicled firsthand).[401] And if an entire society, rulers and subjects alike, collectively refuse to hear preaching, then missionaries must peaceably depart.[402] The Indigenous martyring of preachers justifies war only when the killing is done in hatred of *Christianity*, not of imperial evils. He makes it clear on which side of the line he thinks those killings done by Indigenous Americans fall.[403]

The lodestones of limited ecclesiastical jurisdiction, peaceful evangelization, and Indigenous rights (religious and political) guide Las Casas's reading of

---

396 *Id.*

397 *Id.* at 27; *see also id.* at 300–01 ("[T]he servant who bears the invitation to the wedding feast (that is, the preacher of the gospel) should proclaim the gospel not armed with cannon, like the wolf seeking to kill and rob the sheep, but equipped with a holy way of life and the word of God, risking his life for the spread of the gospel and Christ's glory.").

398 *Id.* at 159, 331; *see also id.* at 337 ("[A] people naturally, or almost naturally, love their original ruler .... Therefore a people would admit this with as much difficulty as they would accept a new religion, especially if a foreigner is substituted for the deposed former lord ....").

399 *Id.* at 120 (citation omitted); *see also id.* at 52 (observing that the Church's Good Friday prayers distinguish between "barbarians[] who are enemies of the Church" and those "who do not bother Christian people").

400 *See id.* at 168–69; *see also id.* at 185; Clayton & Lantigua, *supra* n.128, at 118–20 (excerpting from a primary source).

401 *See* Las Casas, Defense, *supra* n.278, at 186–94; Las Casas, Destruction, *supra* n.192.

402 *See* Las Casas, Defense, *supra* n.278, at 172–73; Clayton & Lantigua, *supra* n.128, at 78–82 (excerpting from Las Casas's theological argument).

403 *See* Lantigua, *supra* n.42, at 171.

Inter caetera.[404] The bull authorizes Castilian supervision of convert Indian rulers, but only for the latter's "protection and jurisdiction."[405] The bull's factual recitations are critical. Because Alexander described the Indians as gentle people and prospective converts, he cannot have meant for them to be "overcome by war."[406] Because Isabella and Ferdinand said they intended to "lead" Indigenous peoples to Christianity, this must mean sincere conversion through peaceful evangelization and not coercion.[407] Thus, *Inter caetera*'s instruction that natives be "subjected" has to mean gently leading them to listen to Christian preaching and embrace the faith—even if a literal reading of the bull "fights back" against this interpretation.[408]

In another law-backed reading, because "a papal rescript favoring one individual should not prejudice the rights of a third party," *Inter caetera* assumes Indian sovereigns' "pre-existing rights and liberties even though it granted 'lordships and jurisdictions' in the Indies to Spain."[409] Indigenous sovereignty can be transferred to the Spanish only upon the consent of the rulers and people because, under yet another legal rule, "what touches all must be approved by all."[410]

---

404 Las Casas was positively enthused about *Inter caetera*, even arranging for its printing. *See* Gutiérrez, *supra* n.125, at 72.

405 Las Casas, Defense, *supra* n.278, at 349.

406 *Id.* at 350.

407 *Id.* at 351, 353–55; *see also Inter caetera*, *supra* n.5, at 74 ("inducere"). Las Casas had interpreted this part of *Inter caetera* similarly in an earlier letter of 1535. *See* Cárdenas Bunsen, *supra* n.189, at 63–64 & n.17.

408 *See Inter caetera*, *supra* n.5, at 73 ("subjicere"). Poole's translation of "repugnaret" as "opposed" is too soft. *Contrast* Las Casas, Defense, supra n.278, at 353, 360 *with* Las Casas, Apologia, *supra* n.384, at 252; *see also* Glen Carman, *On the Pope's Original Intent: Las Casas Reads the Papal Bulls of 1493*, 7 Colonial Lat. Am. Rev. 193, 202 n.2 (1998) (criticizing Poole's word choice).

409 Brian Tierney, The Idea of Natural Rights: Studies on Natural Rights, Natural Law and Church Law 1150–1625 pp. 281–83 (1997) [hereinafter "Natural Rights"] (discussing Las Casas's De Thesauris in Peru); *see also* Las Casas, Disputa, *supra* n.389, at 108; *Inter caetera*, *supra* n.5, at 74 (conferring "dominiis" and "jurisdictionibus"); Valdivia Jiménez, *supra* n.209, at 187 n.57; Adorno, *supra* n.191, at 123 (noting that Las Casas recognized Indian polities, unlike Vitoria, and suggesting that this is because of his focus on law rather than philosophy or theology).

410 Pennington, *supra* n.371, at 103; *see also* Tierney, Natural Rights, *supra* n.409, at 283 (summarizing that Spaniards' right to rule their colonies depends on confirmation that "could only come from the free consent of the Indian people and their rulers"); *id.* at 285 (explaining that rule by foreigners requires unanimous consent); Clayton & Lantigua, *supra* n.128, at 113–15; Dickason, *supra* n.72, at 171–72 (naming Nicholas of Cusa (1401–1464) as this norm's originator).

The whole purpose of imperialism, then, is evangelization, not the accumulation of territory.[411] And the Empire's *Inter caetera*-authorized[412] role is protecting peaceful missions.[413]

Las Casas's contribution was another earthquake whose tremors crossed the sea to Europe. The Valladolid *junta* concluded that conquests were "dangerous to Your Majesty's conscience."[414] The following year, Texcuco Indians declared that much of Mexico still rightly belonged to Indigenous people. The colonial capital's council repeatedly, unsuccessfully asked Charles to censor Las Casas. A decade later, a colonial official reported that friars were anticipating an end to Indian taxation and the restoration of Indigenous sovereignty because evangelization was taking hold.[415] The viceroy of Peru expressed dismay that local clerics were citing Las Casas to brand his every move "tyrannical and unjust," even hiding Indians from imperial tax collectors.[416]

In his last known writing, in 1566, Las Casas asked the new pope, Pius v (r. 1566–1572), to excommunicate anyone who justified either indirect coercion or war against idolatry.[417] Instead, Pius wrote to Philip saying Alexander had

---

411 *See* Las Casas, Defense, *supra* n.278, at 357.

412 Las Casas does not accept any natural-law justification for colonization. *See* Avira & Cruz, *supra* n.197, at 96–97 ("[Q]uite unlike Vitoria, Las Casas concentrates all rights and responsibilities in the Church. ... [T]he defense of the innocents, could justify the war, but not because this constituted an obligation of natural law for all men, but because the innocents were commended to the charge of *the Church* by divine law. ... [T]he papal bull as interpreted by Las Casas was a source only of duties, and that, only for the Christians."). Spanish authority in the West Indies is entirely "subrogated from the Holy See." Valdivia Jiménez, *supra* n.209, at 189, 191.

413 *See* Las Casas, Defense, *supra* n.278, at 179–80. Las Casas specifically mentions his own mission settlement of "*Vera Paz*" (aptly, "True Peace"). *See id.* Some have seen his approach as unrealistic, and indeed, Vera Paz "ended in failure. The Lacandons, a warrior tribe that practiced human sacrifices, ended the experiment with the sacrifice of several newly converted sons and the martyrdom of two Dominicans." Andújar, *supra* n.379, at 84. But then, Andújar's evaluation depends on a meaning of success that excludes martyrdom. *Contrast with* The Mission (Warner Bros. 1986) (powerfully depicting the fictionalized martyrdom of seventeenth-century Jesuits defending peaceful Guaraní missions from the Portuguese).

414 Urbano, *supra* n.318, at 245 (quoting a letter from the Council of the Indies to Charles v).

415 *See* Hanke, Struggle, *supra* n.151, at 156–58.

416 *See id.* at 163.

417 *See* Clayton & Lantigua, *supra* n.128, at 121 (quoting Las Casas's petition, which also passionately refers to "those Indians whose rights I have defended till my death"); Stogre, *supra* n.86, at 94.

granted lands to Isabella and Ferdinand for evangelization, and doing this well would extend the Empire's colonies.[418]

5.1 *Evaluating Las Casas's Reading of* Inter caetera: *Creativity unto Radicalism*

By the later stages of his life, Las Casas was demanding the return of Incan sovereignty and requesting papal condemnation of Innocent's opinions about indirect coercion. How did he arrive at these radical positions? Biographically, by witnessing conquest up close. Atrocities were real for him in a way that they were merely abstract for many other Spanish intellectuals, including even Vitoria. Intellectually, Las Casas fought back by **inverting** *Inter caetera* into a defense of Indigenous rights. He reinterpreted its text using theologically derived principles—namely, basic legal norms, peaceful evangelization, and respect for Indigenous rights. Las Casas uniquely cast Alexander as the protector of Indian freedom against violent *conquistadores*, exploitative tax collectors, and even coercive churchmen.

His interpretation persuaded neither most Spaniards nor Pius, although it inspired subversion by Indians and friars alike. It also demonstrates the flexibility that contributed to *Inter caetera*'s influence on generations of Spanish intellectuals, even as decades of conquest turned into centuries of colonial rule.

5.2 Inter caetera *Assessed: Alexander's Enduring Role in Spanish Imperialism*

In 1581–82, around fifteen years after Las Casas's death, explorer Sarmiento de Gamboa sailed to the Straits of Magellan on the Americas' southernmost tip. One of his captains, Diego Flores, protested that he "didn't see what title the king had to the Indies anyway." Gamboa unconvincingly listed off various justifications for empire. Finally, he showed Flores *Inter caetera* and "sternly warned him that anyone who contradicted this title contradicted the power of the pope and soiled the royal conscience." Flores yielded.[419]

418 Pope Pius v, *Al Rey de Espana, Para Que El Yugo de Cristo Sea Suave a Los Indios* (Aug. 17, 1568), *reprinted in* Colección de Bulas, Breves y Otros Documentos Relativos a la Iglesia de America y Filipinas 104 (Francisco Javier Hernaez ed., Kraus Reprint Ltd., 1964) (1879). Pius also promoted the development of an Indigenous clergy, but did not directly invoke Indigenous rights. *See* Stogre, *supra* n.86, at 95–96.

419 Hanke, Struggle, *supra* n.151, at 171–72; *accord id.* at 148 (quoting *conquistador* Gonzalo Jiménez de Quesada (*c.*1495–1579): "The western Indies belong to Spain ... by the concession of the popes, who are vicars of God throughout the universe.").

Paz, Vitoria, and Las Casas did not: they critiqued Spanish imperialism from within. Many agreed with them. And yet, five centuries after the *Requerimiento* was first chanted in alien tongues along the beaches and in the jungles—at Indigenous listeners who reacted to news of the bull with incredulity, thinking Pope Alexander drunk and King Ferdinand *el Católico* insane—how do we assess *Inter caetera*? The Vatican was certainly right in 2023 in not repeating the claim that the bull was a nonentity a mere thirteen months after Alexander issued it.[420] Before even Burgos.

Whether the new Vatican statement is ultimately satisfactory is a question for further Indigenous-Catholic dialogue. Its authors had many considerations to take into account, including half a millennium of traumas and triumphs throughout formerly colonized lands, profound changes in interrelations among societies and cultures, and the tremendous benefits many (including myself and, certainly, Vatican officials) believe Christian evangelization brought to Indigenous peoples—especially those who were brutalized first by Indigenous empires like the Aztecs, Inca, and Maya.[421] Vatican officials also had to weigh ongoing questions surrounding the same matters that vexed the Salamancans: humanitarian intervention, self-determination, and cultural relativism. They know far more about the world and its peoples than did Alexander when he signed that fateful bull, so their task was far more difficult.

All that I have to offer is this: *Inter caetera* was an enduring part of Spanish imperialism. Contrary to the oversimplifications of modern critics, it did not contribute to English (or U.S.) colonization. But despite what has been argued by some overly defensive Catholics, and even some careful scholars, Alexander *did* intend to authorize some conquest. And in spite of the forceful attacks leveled against *Inter caetera* by Vitoria's natural-law theories, its significance endured. Many—colonizers and colonized alike—always understood Spain's rule over Indigenous lands to come straight from Alexander's hand.

420 *See* Dicasteries for Culture and Education and for Promoting Integral Human Development, *supra* n.38.

421 *See* Andújar, *supra* n.379, at 75 (noting that many Indians displayed "massive and passionate adherence to the *Pax Hispanica*").

www.ingramcontent.com/pod-product-compliance
Lightning Source LLC
Chambersburg PA
CBHW031333230926
51848CB00001B/212
* 9 7 8 9 0 0 4 6 8 1 4 2 2 *